THE TOP 11 OF EVERYTHING SPURS

Tottenham Hotspur

IT'S NOT TRIVIA, IT'S MORE IMPORTANT THAN THAT

Written by
Alison Ratcliffe

Text editors
Paul Simpson, Helen Rodiss,
Michaela Bushell

Production
Ian Cranna, Tim Oldham,
Tim Harrison

Cover and Book design
Sharon O'Connor

Cover image
David Oliver/Getty Images

Thanks to
Simon Kanter, Mark Ellingham,
Andrew Lockett, David Francis,
Stuart Randall, Mo Brittain,
Paul Brittain, Mat Snow

Printed in Spain by
Graphy Cems

This edition published
July 2005 was prepared by
Haymarket Network for
Rough Guides Ltd,
80 Strand, London, WC2R ORL

Distributed by the
Penguin Group
Penguin Books Ltd,
27 Wrights Lane,
London W8 5TZ

A catalogue record for this
book is available from the
British Library

ISBN 1-8435-3558-0

ROUGH
GUIDES

Contents

D1412988

11 ABSOLUTE BEST MOMENTS

Oh happy days...

1. When the Double came to Tottenham 1961

There was a queue for the bingo hall but otherwise Tottenham High Road was empty. "No one will want to come out and look at a couple of cups," thought Danny Blanchflower. An hour and a half later, the street was teeming. Around 100,000 delirious Spurs fans crammed the pavement. They dangled out of windows, clung to trees. The bingo hall band serenaded the Double-winners' open-top bus as it passed and the bingo-ites roared them on. Danny never realised what it really meant to win the Double until that procession. "That day summed the whole season up. A season of victory and crowds, a season for Tottenham Hotspur and football to remember."

2. When Mackay grabbed Bremner 1966

He sat in the gym lifting 28lb weights on his injured leg for days on end. He spent two years dieting to sustain match weight. Twice he faced the prospect of never playing again. Then, in August 1966, along came Billy Bremner and deliberately kicked Dave Mackay's twice-broken leg. Immortalised in the photograph is a very hard man, who is very, very annoyed. Mackay hates the picture. He thinks it portrays him as a bully. But only Mackay, a man of formidable brawn but scrupulous fairness, could worry he would be condemned for intimidating the dastardly Bremner.

3. When Jürgen dived 1994

The English tabloid press tamed by a German. The sweet irony. Evasive answers and flat denials they were prepared for, but with Jürgen's beguiling self-mockery they simpered like teenage girls. They'd fallen for him when he asked for directions to the nearest diving school at his signing-on press conference. When he led the team in a communal headlong dive after his first Spurs goal they were in love. The goal set Spurs on their way to beating Sheffield Wednesday by four goals to three, that most Tottenham of scores, and it launched the season of Ossie and the Famous Five.

4. When Alfie sat on the ball 1975

What would your worst nightmare sound like? A staunch Gooner in charge of Spurs? Relegation looming? Losing to Arsenal (1-0, naturally)? And in the last game of the season you have to beat Don Revie's Leeds to stay up? Welcome to April 1975. But out of the depths of fear, Cyril Knowles scores two. Returning hero Martin Chivers adds a third. Leeds pull one back, but Alfie Conn dribbles past three men and scores. Then he sits on the ball. And beckons to Billy Bremner. The other Spurs players are furious. It's time to seal the win and tiptoe quietly out of the room, not dangle a bleeding piece of meat in front of the rottweiler. The Spurs fans, though, are ecstatic. It's the two-fingered gesture par excellence. "Tell him," says Bremner to Perryman. "Tell him you're going to win the game, but he's not going to finish it."

5. When Greavsie and Bobby danced 1969

West Ham's visit to Spurs in April 1969 was dragging on. Jimmy Greaves scored the only goal of the game. The crowd got bored and so did Greavsie. So while another scintillating attack wasn't being launched, he and Bobby Moore linked arms and did a ceilidh-style jig. The referee booked them.

6. When the fans met Ossie and Ricky 1978

Two very different welcomes awaited Ossie Ardiles and Ricardo Villa on their move to England. First, Peter Taylor brought a fake thumb to a pre-season photo shoot, which came away when Ricky Villa shook his hand. Then they played their first game at White Hart Lane. Forty-eight thousand Spurs fans made like 77,000 frenzied Argentinians: the roar was immense and ticker tape erupted from around the ground. Argentina's World Cup win of a month before was recreated; the Maracana came to N17. Newly promoted Spurs had inexplicably signed English football's first two global superstars. It was the beginning of European glory, cups, and valiant assaults on the title. The game itself ended 4-1 to Aston Villa, but that's Spurs.

7. When Mackay and Henry couldn't find the ball 1962

Snow and army sides. There's not much of either about any more and European competition is the poorer for it. Dukla Prague at White Hart Lane in the European Cup was one of those glory glory nights. Dave Mackay, Ron Henry and the Dukla Prague outside-right all fell in a heap. When they dusted themselves off, there was no sign of the ball. Clearly, the only option was to fashion footballs out of snow and start a snowball fight.

8. Nayim from the halfway line 1995

Seaman lost the ball in the glare of the floodlights apparently. Whatever. There were ten seconds to go before the semi-final of the 1995 Cup Winners' Cup tie between

11. ALL-TIME SPURS XI

Pat Jennings

Alf Ramsey   Mike England   Cyril Knowles

Danny
Blanchflower   Dave Mackay   Ron Burgess

Cliff Jones   Glenn Hoddle

Alan Gilzean

Jimmy Greaves

This is essentially a 3-5-2 with some cheating for typographic reasons and to squeeze in talented players in the same position who are just too good to leave out

Arsenal and Real Zaragoza was decided on penalties. Nayim cocked that glorious ball from the halfway line and we were treated to the now familiar sight of Seaman treading water. That the scorer was an ex-Spur was good; that it was an ex-Spur who, for all his flashes of skill, never quite cut it, somehow made it even better. Seaman went and blubbed in the dressing room and a classic chant was born.

9. When Steffen Freund scored 2001
It was Friday 13th. The thunder thundered, the rain pitched down and the Spurs reserve team pitched up 15 minutes late. It was to be an historic evening. In the 77th minute, with Spurs leading Stevenage by five goals to one, Steffen Iversen released Steffen Freund on the right. Freund delicately chipped a defender and the ball bounced, agonisingly, towards goal… A defender was closing it down… It was heading for the post… The referee blew his whistle and pointed to the centre-spot. On 13 July 2001, after 916 days and 87 matches in a Tottenham shirt, the Football Genius had scored. As for whether it really crossed the line, well, let's not split hairs.

10. When Graham met Charlie 1986
"Who put Charlie in the stand?" went up the cry from the Spurs fans in the Clock End on New Year's Day in 1986. Despite having just watched Graham Roberts administer

an Ali uppercut of a tackle, sending Charlie Nicholas sailing into row Z, the Gooners seemed not to remember.

11. When Diego played for Spurs 1986
It's incongruous even to imagine Diego Maradona on the Tottenham High Road. But a sell-out White Hart Lane crowd clearly saw him trot out in that Hummel shirt with the arrows just above the 'Holsten', juggle the ball by the byline and volley it sweetly onto the head of local lad and honest workhorse Mark Falco. (It didn't go in; the story's not quite perfect.) Clive Allen dispatched a winner, Inter were beaten and those present at Ossie Ardiles's 1986 testimonial went home with a warm feeling.

ALMOST SIGNINGS

11 players who didn't quite put pen to paper

1. Diego Maradona
'Spurs Chase Diego' – a tabloid headline from yesteryear. Diego was rumoured to be following in Ossie's footsteps in the late 1980s. The next Argentinian to sign for Spurs was Mauricio Taricco.

2. Michel Platini
"I had proposals from clubs like Arsenal and Tottenham and my wife wanted to go to London. I decided against it because you play too many games in England. But there is a small part of me that wonders what life in England would have been like."

3. Johan Cruyff
Terry Neill had everything in place: Cruyff was keen and Neill had secured sponsorship to finance the deal. But when the board heard of it via the *Daily Express* they weren't impressed and vetoed the transfer.

4. Ronaldo
July 2004: "Frank Arnesen at Tottenham makes me think of England again and it would be ideal to work under him." Presumably not while he's at Spurs, though.

5. Zinedine Zidane
Spurs took a long hard look at him when he was playing for Bordeaux but decided not to sign him on the grounds he was "too wooden".

6. Andriy Shevchenko
Agent Sandor Varga said Shevchenko "favoured a move to England and was excited by the prospect of linking up again with Sergei Rebrov".

7. Roman Abramovich
Famously checked out Tottenham before mysteriously deciding the Fulham Road was a better bet. Daniel Levy denies ever having had an approach from Abramovich or his representatives.

8. Bobby Moore
Nearly crossed to north London just before the 1966 World Cup after a wage dispute with West Ham.

9. Rivaldo
Wrote to Glenn Hoddle explaining his decision to choose Milan over Spurs.

10. Edgar Davids
Spurs reportedly offered Davids a £6-million, two-year deal to sign from Juventus in May 2004. "I've had two offers from England that I like," he said. "But I especially like the one from Tottenham."

11. Fernando Morientes
"At the moment we're in negotiations with Real Madrid," said Hoddle in August 2002. "We're totally genuine. Sometimes you get what you want in life and sometimes you don't. You have to keep shopping if the groceries run out and go on to the next one."

ALWAYS IN THE CD CHANGER...

11 musical tributes (see www.cherryred.co.uk for more anthems)

1. The Football Match 1908
This descriptive fantasia for the piano by Ezra Read was written when Tottenham entered the Football League "in admiration of their many gallant games".

2. Tip Top Tottenham Hotspur, The Totnamites 1961
Tip top Tottenham Hotspur, the greatest team of the year
Tip top Tottenham Hotspur, raise your glasses and give them a cheer
Hooray for the double, and let's live it up/One for the league and another one for the cup...

3. Spurs' 1967 FA Cup success inspired them to quite prodigious outpourings

Bye Bye Blackbird, Terry Venables and the Spurs squad
Maybe It's Because I'm A Londoner, Alan Mullery, Cyril Knowles and the Spurs squad
When Irish Eyes Are Smiling Pat Jennings, Joe Kinnear and the Spurs squad
Strolling, Jimmy Greaves and the 1967 Spurs squad
It's A Grand Old Team, the Spurs squad
Glory Glory Hallelujah, Terry Venables and the Spurs squad

4. Nice One Cyril 1973

The Cockerel Chorus make the first Spurs record to hit the charts, reaching number 14.

5. Hot Spurs Boogie 1973

To coincide with the League Cup final.
Tottenham Hotspur, Tottenham Hotspur is our team
Tottenham Hotspur, the best you've ever seen
Tottenham Hotspur, come and watch us play
Tottenham Hotspur, we're winning all the way
Sing, shout, let's call out
Tottenham Hotspur, Tottenham Hotspur

6. Amigos O'Lane 1978

A tribute to Ossie Ardiles and Ricky Villa.

7. Ossie's Dream 1981

Chas & Dave's classic made it all the way to number five. The first verse is still a favourite Cup chant at the Lane. Less often heard is verse number three...
We are the boys of Keithie's army
And we're marching off to war
We're sending our soldiers to Wembley
Under General Burkinshaw

> "WE ARE THE BOYS OF KEITHIE'S ARMY, AND WE'RE MARCHING OFF TO WAR." VERSE THREE OF OSSIE'S DREAM

8. Tottenham Tottenham 1982

Chas & Dave's FA Cup final song spent seven weeks in the charts, peaking at number 19.
And just the touch of magic there you're about to see
Like when Ossie's dream came true
Stevie can't wait to hold the cup again
Won't be satisfied until it's in his hands
He'll hold it up for everyone to see it
Then we'll hear the boys of our bands

9. Diamond Lights 1987

They called themselves Glenn and Chris, presumably because a silly name like 'Hoddle and Waddle' would have detracted from their standing in the music biz.

10. Hot Shot Tottenham by Chas & Dave 1987

11. When the Year Ends In One & The Victory Song 1991

We're off to Wembley 'cos we beat the Arsenal. Chas & Dave: still going strong.

THE ARSENAL HALL OF INFAMY

"Parking is difficult enough in London without so many meters being occupied by Arsenal players slumped over the steering wheel." Mike Langley, Sunday People

1. Game of tag

On 2 April 2005, Arsenal loanee Jermaine Pennant plays for Birmingham against Spurs with an electronic tag around his ankle following release from prison. He had been convicted of drink driving and driving while disqualified. Pennant is bidding to make it a hat-trick of offences: he had just finished a drink driving rehabilitation course when arrested.

2. United we fall

Arsenal receive a record £175,000 fine for failing to control their players (ie for rubbing Ruud Van Nistelrooy's muzzle in it in a quite unnecessary fashion after he missed a penalty) during their 0-0 draw with Manchester United at Old Trafford in September 2003. Though it was Martin Keown who impressed most with his demented monkey routine, Lauren received the biggest punishment: a £40,000 fine and a four-game ban for "forcibly pushing Van Nistelrooy in the back following the final whistle". Keown was fined £20,000 and suspended for three games, while Patrick Vieira and Ray Parlour were fined £20,000 and £10,000 respectively and banned for a game.

3. Bad discipline

In 1998/99 Arsenal finished with the worst disciplinary record in the Premiership – ten red cards and 81 yellows.

4. Hong Kung Phooey

In May 1995, Ray Parlour manhandles a Hong Kong cabbie while on a club tour. He is fined £170 by authorities. Arsenal hit him for two weeks' wages and a £3,200 bonus.

5. Bungling George
George Graham is found guilty of misconduct by the FA, and given a worldwide ban, following accusations in October 1994 that he accepted bungs in the transfers of John Jensen and Pal Lydersen.

6. Pizza parlour
In November 1993, Ray Parlour can't resist the siren call of a fire extinguisher in a pizza parlour (and is duly "admonished").

7. Disunited
In October 1990, a brawl erupts during Arsenal's game against Man United. Arsenal are fined £50,000, which they finance by fining Nigel Winterburn, Michael Thomas, David Rocastle, Paul Davis, Anders Limpar and George Graham two weeks' wages.

8. Banged up
In May 1990, Tony Adams parks his car head-on against a wall and is lucky to live to claim another offside. His 56-day prison term gives him time to reflect on the £1,000 fine he receives from the FA for flashing V signs at opposition fans.

9. Bottled out
In 1989, star in the making Paul Vaessen admits to a newspaper that he resorted to burglary to feed his heroin habit. This in the same year Kenny Sansom tells a Sunday paper about the season that passed him by "in a nightmare of empty bottles".

10. High fives
Between 1981 and 1988, five Arsenal players are punished for drink driving. Charlie Nicholas is banned three times; Tony Woodcock is picked up just a short mazy drive from The Royal Courts of Justice; Raphael Meade collects a one-year ban to go with the fortnight's jail term received for obstructing police trying to arrest his friend; Alan Sunderland is banned for a year, but cleared of blame for the deaths of two pedestrians who stepped in front of his car; while Graham Rix's drunken drive sees him relieved of the captaincy.

11. Holiday pranks
June 1987. Take two Arsenal players and one Algarve resort, add a few snifters and sit back and wait for the fisticuffs. Portuguese police told Viv Anderson and Rhys Wilmot they'd been very naughty boys.

BEST FOREIGN SIGNINGS

It's all about enriching the game…

1. Osvaldo Ardiles

What a treat for English fans: a player who could control a ball without looking at it. The partnership between Ardiles and Hoddle looked as though they had honed it together from a tender age. Ardiles had the cultural intelligence to settle quickly. But the atmosphere in Britain during the Falklands War was such that he had to go on loan to Paris Saint-Germain and missed the 1982 FA Cup win. Sadly the injuries that plagued him on his return meant fans never really saw him at his best again.

2. Jürgen Klinsmann

A ravenous student of cultures, he'd already sounded out how the British media works by the time he appeared at his signing-on press conference. The phrase "It takes time to get used to the Premiership" never passed his lips. He had his perfect partner waiting on the pitch in Teddy Sheringham. He scored on his debut, again on his home debut and finished the season with 29 goals. Two seasons later he returned, heroically, to pluck Spurs from the relegation mire.

3. David Ginola

He was inconsistent, but you just can't buy that kind of player without a built-in waywardness function. It's a testament to Ginola's ability that he won a PFA Player of the Year award in a George Graham team. Remember the chest-down, the drag-back and the explosive dribble? And if he wasn't creating anything, at least he was keeping two members of the opposition sidetracked.

4. Ricky Villa

Is it harsh to wonder what Ricky Villa's legend status would be if he hadn't scored that glorious 1981 Cup final winner? Certainly he wouldn't have had the same profile, but White Hart Lane would still have loved him, as we've loved a hundred flair men, who dazzled in one game and disappeared the next. Like Ossie he left when opposition crowds began to barrack him over the Falklands conflict (he headed to Fort Lauderdale Strikers in Florida) but unlike Ossie, Villa would never have the confidence or the resilience to return.

5. Erik Thorstvedt

Erik Thorstvedt? Fifth best foreign Spurs player? But Ardiles aside, no other overseas player has established himself so consistently for so long (177 appearances). He was suffering knee injuries when Ian Walker began to nudge him out of the side and if Walker sometimes hit greater heights, his scary moments came more frequently.

6. Gica Popescu

He was "so gifted he could make anything look easy," says Teddy Sheringham, "so quick in thought and deed he sees situations before they occur and snuffs them out with supreme skill." The football Spurs played under Ardiles was probably too harebrained to take full advantage of Popescu, while under Gerry Francis it was too crude. Spurs have been scratching around for a player of his ilk ever since.

7. Fredi Kanoute

There's a top-class striker inside Fredi. You just never know when he's going to come out to play or how to tempt him out more often. He can score breathtaking goals (like the bicycle kick on his debut against Leeds), has the most gossamer touch for a big fella, can hold a ball up and lay off a perfect pass. Or he can be a waste of space.

8. Steffen Freund

Perhaps the phrase 'most influential', rather than 'best' is more apt for Steffen Freund. When it comes to ball skills there's no shortage of players from home or abroad to surpass him, but few whose absence will leave such a big hole.

9. Christian Ziege

The chief Ziege gripe was he didn't do his share of graft (see how Gooner Graham rubbed off on us!). But there were plenty of moments when he showed the class that got him a place in the World Cup final, his top-drawer free kicks among them. Injuries disrupted the flow until the daddy of them all – the one against Charlton that left a 12-inch scar and which could have been fatal – ultimately wrote him off.

10. Nayim

The stunner at Southend in the League Cup (he flicked it over his head and slotted it through the keeper's legs) and the hat-trick against Manchester City… Nayim could be pretty special. El Tel's Barça protege had the full box of continental skills plus a fair-size dollop of inconsistency.

11. Stéphane Dalmat (for three games)

When Fredi Kanoute scored a hat-trick against Palace in the Cup and wasn't voted man of the match by the Spurs fans, the press said the crowd had snubbed him for playing in the African Nations Cup. They conveniently ignored the scintillating game of football produced by the actual vote-winner Stéphane Dalmat. His skill, swerves and shimmies and indomitable physique added up to something very special. He'd produced something similar in a previous game, and repeated it to a lesser extent in a third. But in 25 appearances, that was all the super Stéphane we got.

BEST GOALKEEPERS

Last line of defence, first of attack

1. Pat Jennings 1964-77

"If Jennings had been available on that memorable occasion when the Romans met the Etruscans, Horatius surely would have had to be satisfied with a seat on the substitutes bench," wrote Eric Todd in the *Guardian* in 1972. Spurs had just lost 2-1 to Leeds United in the FA Cup – not 6 or 7-1, as the score would have read with a 'normal' goalkeeper. That Jennings was still up an Irish mountainside felling trees, having never been near a football pitch, 18 months before making his Spurs debut is all part of

> THAT JENNINGS WAS UP AN IRISH MOUNTAIN FELLING TREES 18 MONTHS EARLIER IS PART OF THE MYSTIQUE

the mystique. The track record is always worth reeling off one more time: 590 appearances for Spurs, 119 Northern Ireland caps, one UEFA Cup, one FA Cup, two League Cups, one Football Writers' Player of the Year award, one Players' Player of the Year award, an OBE and an MBE. And some trophies at Arsenal, but we don't talk about that, do we Mr Burkinshaw?

2. Ted Ditchburn 1946-59

Boxing and goalkeeping had more in common in the 1950s, so it may have helped Edwin Ditchburn, the son of a pro fighter, that he once considered becoming one. His agility on the line, powerful close-range smothering, point-blank saves and lightning reflexes would have been handy in the ring. As would his uncuddly relationship with opposing centre-forwards. Better than Jennings, according to Terry Venables, Ditchburn was ever-present for 247 games between April 1948 and March 1954, taking in promotion to Division One and the push-and-run championship. For some strange reason, he was a far less imposing performer in England games and consequently he played in only eight of them. But only Jennings and Steve Perryman have pulled on a Spurs shirt more times.

3. Bill Brown 1959-66

One club's inability to pay for their new floodlights is another's goalkeeping legend. Dundee needed the £16,500 and Spurs needed a replacement for Ted Ditchburn. Brown was not Ted's equal but he was class. While his Double-winning team-mates disappeared up the other end of the pitch for long spells, Brown remained alert to every twist of the game. Sharp shot-stopping and canny positioning were his assets, and if he was occasionally dodgy on crosses, Maurice Norman would clean up.

4. Ray Clemence 1981-87

Clemence spent his first season at Spurs acclimatising to playing behind a less sturdy backline than he was used to. History will record him as a Liverpool man who won five titles, three European Cups, two UEFA Cups, an FA Cup and a League Cup in 11 seasons at Anfield. But his slightly erratic first season with Spurs – when his clanger saw the club exit the Cup Winners' Cup against Barcelona – culminated in an FA Cup win. Clemence was back to his best and the sure-handed, Anfield-style sweeper-keeper went on to shepherd the Spurs back line with authority.

5. Paul Robinson 2003-

After ducking Kasey Keller's clearances for two seasons, the good folk of the East and West stands must enjoy watching Paul Robinson's passes, goal-kicks and clearances unerringly find their man. And who needs midfield cover when you've got a shot-stopper of Robbo's class? If Hans Segers can make Robinson a little more confident plucking high balls from teeming penalty areas, who knows where Robinson's assault on Tottenham's list of goalkeeping greats will end?

6. Erik Thorstvedt 1989-94

Thorstvedt gifted Nigel Clough the winner on his debut at home to Forest in front of a live TV audience. Following the trauma of Bobby Mimms, it seemed the ghost of Clemence was still haunting the penalty area. Thorstvedt continued to look shaky, dropping a clanger at Charlton. Then he brought down Alan Shearer on the edge of the area at Southampton. But the referee didn't send him off, Thorstvedt kept a clean sheet, threw his gloves to the fans, and the legend of Erik the Viking was born.

7. Ian Walker 1990-2001

Chants of "Ian the Saxon" confirmed Walker as the Viking's successor. Capable? Yes. A good shot-stopper? Certainly. Walker veered between accomplished and slightly suspect. He didn't always command his area and his positioning could be dubious.

He impressed enough to play for England but was blamed for Gianfranco Zola's goal for Italy and never capped again. George Graham eventually went for Neil Sullivan.

8. George Clawley 1899-1903
A three-times Southern League winner with Southampton St Mary's, Clawley also had a hand in Spurs' first Southern League win. He played in all Spurs' games as they claimed the FA Cup in 1901, proving his reliability and aerial prowess in 186 games.

9. Barry Daines 1971-81
Daines was so good, Keith Burkinshaw sold Pat Jennings. Fans weren't convinced and Burkinshaw later admitted his error. Given a little self-confidence Daines might have been a solid successor to Jennings. Spurs were relegated when Jennings was injured in 1976/77, but it was no fault of Daines, who played well as Spurs were immediately promoted. Back in the top flight, Daines was never convinced of his own abilities. By now, neither was Burkinshaw, who drafted in Milija Aleksic in 1981.

10. Kasey Keller 2001-04
Keller was a handy shot-stopper and by all accounts a lovely fella, but couldn't kick for toffee. But chanting "YooooEssAy" at Kasey was always fun.

11. Tony Parkes 1984-87
The 1984 UEFA Cup final against Anderlecht has ended one apiece. Danny Thomas misses his penalty. The crowd chants his name but Thomas sits head in hands. "Then it was on to Tony Parkes," recalls Garth Crooks. "It was 'Can he pull us out of it?' He was reserve keeper. He was a good keeper, but he was never ever going to be a star." Parkes saves Morten Olsen's penalty – and then Arnor Gudjohnsen's. Spurs win. "It came at the right height, a lovely height to make it look spectacular," admits Parkes. "We all like a bit of glory and I must admit I made it look a better save than it was."

BEST WINS
It's an absolute goal-fest. In order of margin of victory

1. 13-2	v Crewe Alexandra (h)	3 Feb 1960	FA Cup
2. 9-0	v Worksop (h)	15 Jan 1923	FA Cup
3. 9-0	v Keflavik (h)	28 Sept 1971	UEFA Cup
4. 9-0	v Bristol Rovers (h)	22 Oct 1977	League
5. 9-1	v Tranmere Rovers (h)	12 Jan 1953	FA Cup
6. 8-0	v Southampton (h)	28 Mar 1936	League

7. 8-0 v Drogheda (h)   28 Sept 1983   UEFA Cup
8. 9-2 v Nott'm Forest (h)   29 Sept 1962   League
9. 8-1 v Burnley (h)   1 Sept 1930   League
10. 8-1 v Gornik Zabrze (h)   20 Sept 1961   European Cup
11. 7-0 v Burnley (h)   7 Sept 1968   League

BEYOND THE CALL OF DUTY

11 tales of true devotion to the cause

1. Bill Nick's day used to consist of training in the morning, administration in the afternoon and scouting in the evening. Home-time was usually gone midnight – so long as he wasn't flying up to Scotland to watch a lower division evening game and travelling back through the night.

2. Arthur Rowe, a fervent Tottenham fan as well as manager, was so overwrought about the team's declining fortunes he suffered a breakdown. Hostile directors may well also have played their part.

3. Who'd be Spurs manager? Rowe's successor, **Jimmy Anderson**, also became ill with the stress of Spurs' fading fortunes, resigning after Spurs took just three points from the opening seven games of 1958/59.

4. Alan Mullery, who had previously played on through the pain of a persistent pelvic injury, knocked himself out heading the goal that sealed the 1972 UEFA Cup.

5. Bill Brown took a hefty knock against Slovan Bratislava in the 1963 Cup Winners' Cup quarter-final, but with his nose plastered up, his heroics kept the score down to 2-0, paving the way for a Spurs win in the return.

6. Mike England's dodgy knees meant he often played in considerable pain.

7. Though son George had fallen seriously ill with leukaemia, **Gary Lineker** still scored 35 goals in 50 games in 1991/92.

8. Cliff Jones's fearlessness perpetually got him into scrapes. In Spurs' 7-0 win against Burnley in September 1968 he headed a goal and the post too, knocking himself out. He recalls he "couldn't do a lot with the ball" after that, which pleased Bill Nick as it forced him to pass it more often.

9. Feel-no-pain hard man **Bobby Smith** played on despite painful swollen ankles…

10. … and he also played in the 1961 FA Cup final after painkilling injections for his twisted knee.

11. Danny Blanchflower helped Spurs win the 1961 FA Cup final even though his father was dying in hospital.

THE BUTTERFLY EFFECT: HOW DIFFERENT IT MIGHT HAVE BEEN
How the fickle hand of fate takes charge

1. A young lad who'd travelled from Wales for a training-ground trial was about to head home after being rejected. Before setting off, he called by White Hart Lane to see the 'A' team and it happened they were a man short. He was asked if he'd fill in at half-back and did so well Spurs kept him on… for 16 years. Ron Burgess became an all-time great and inspired the club to Second and First Division championships. As Watford manager, he spotted Pat Jennings in an international youth tournament. After nurturing him for a year, Burgess sold him to old team-mate Bill Nicholson.

2. Spurs owe an eternal debt of gratitude to Ted Drake: he was responsible for four trophy wins and some of the most glorious football in the club's history. The Chelsea boss couldn't ignore the glowing scouting reports dropping on his desk about young Hearts left-half Dave Mackay. He went to see for himself but on his return told the press that Reading's Sylvan Anderton, a player he'd had his eye on, was a far better footballer. So Mackay signed for Spurs, where, according to Bill Nicholson and many of the Double side, he made a good team great. Spurs' all-time top scorer Jimmy Greaves says that if Mackay had signed for Chelsea he would probably have stayed at Stamford Bridge.

3. While Ted Drake was buying Sylvan Anderton in preference to Dave Mackay, Bill Nick was buying Dave Mackay because he couldn't sign Mel Charles. Mel, brother of John, had been Nicholson's first choice. But, as if proof were needed that fate was at work, Charles snubbed Spurs in favour of Arsenal.

4. Fourteen thousand people wedged into Spurs' Northumberland Park ground for a Woolwich Arsenal game in 1898. Around 80 fans tried to use the roof of a refreshment bar as overspill. The bar collapsed, five fans needed medical treatment, though it could easily have been worse. The incident proved Spurs couldn't go on at

Northumberland Park and the club began the search for a new location. White Hart Lane was built on a site owned by the brewers Charringtons just up the road and Spurs played their first game there against Notts County on 4 September 1899.

5. Circuses, ballets and jaunts out in Moscow. That's where it all began. At the end of the 1958/59 season Bill Nicholson took the team on tour to Russia. "I am sure that trip accelerated the team spirit, understanding and telepathy that developed between us as players and friends," says Dave Mackay. "Football-wise, that's when we clicked", agrees Cliff Jones. In 1958/59 Spurs had finished 18th. In the season following the Russian tour, they came third. Then came the Double.

6. Immediate promotion back to the top flight. It all came down to a John Duncan shoulder charge. It was 1977/78 and Spurs were intent on playing their way back up. Goals and wins began to flow. But this was Spurs, and at the crunch they dried up: two draws, a defeat, a win, but another two draws. When Hull City came to the Lane on the penultimate day of the season Spurs had to beat them. A footballing famine of a game, it was still 0-0 in the dying seconds. "A cross came into the end of the box," says Duncan. "There was no way I was going to get it. It was the keeper's ball all the way." Duncan shoulder-charged the keeper. "It was a free kick. I took my chance it wouldn't be given." The ball fell to Perryman, who scored. Promotion was mathematically clinched with a 0-0 draw at Southampton on the last day, but, says Duncan, "If we hadn't won that game we wouldn't have gone up. Simple as that."

7. On a pre-season tour of Holland in 1977, Ipswich striker Trevor Whymark broke his leg. Bobby Robson was forced to spend the money earmarked to buy Pat Jennings on a centre-forward. Meanwhile, Terry Neill had called from Arsenal and Jennings, bizarrely told he could leave by Spurs, gave his word he would go to Highbury if the Ipswich move fell through. Robson is convinced Jennings would have allowed Ipswich to win the title. Instead, Jennings spent eight seasons on the dark side – still on top form – and won FA Cup and Cup Winners' Cup medals.

8. If it wasn't for a short-sighted referee 104 years ago, we might be spared those knowing smiles and assertions that Spurs' name isn't on the Cup this season because the year doesn't end in a one. In the FA Cup third round in 1901, Spurs travelled to play bruisers Reading. The Royals took an early lead only for Spurs to equalise against the run of play. Then Spurs keeper George Clawley fumbled a shot and full-back Sandy Tait punched the ball off the line.

> PROMOTION BACK TO THE TOP FLIGHT. IT ALL CAME DOWN TO A JOHN DUNCAN SHOULDER CHARGE

The referee was probably unsighted and Tait got away with it. Spurs lived to take Reading back to White Hart Lane, where they won 3-0. Their name was on the Cup.

9. The next 'year-with-a-one' Cup win hinged on an even pettier quirk of fate. In 1921, Spurs were threatening to crumble away to Southend United in the third round. The penalty awarded to Southend ten minutes before half-time looked set to tip Spurs over the edge. But an argument erupted between the referee and the Shrimpers' Albert Fairclough over the positioning of the ball on the spot. The exasperated Fairclough hammered the ball wide and Spurs went on to win 4-1.

10. There were rumours it was all premeditated of course, but according to Terry Neill, his resignation from Spurs was prompted by disgust at chairman Sidney Wale's treatment of faithful Spurs fan Fred Rhye. Seventy-year-old widower Fred was the faithful dog at Spurs' heel. The players all knew him. When the team went on tour to Canada, New Zealand, Fiji and Australia in the summer of 1976, Fred was the only fan booked to go out. Despite Fred's protestations, Neill insisted he should travel to the airport on the Spurs coach. But Neill later found Fred crying: Wale had ordered him off the coach. Neill says he was close to resigning on the spot. He eventually left after the tour. There were other factors of course, but for better or for worse, Neill was on his way back to Highbury.

11. Did John Pratt's broken nose win the 1972 UEFA Cup for Spurs? It led to the recall of Alan Mullery from his loan exile at Fulham. Mullers returned to captain the team, clinch the semi-final with a 20-yarder against Milan at the San Siro and score the winning header in the final.

CELEBRITY FANS TO BE PROUD OF

Points awarded for celebrity quality and/or loyalty

1. Paul Whitehouse Comic star of the *Fast Show* and *Harry Enfield and Chums*. A local lad and devoted Spur.

2. Chas & Dave Their contribution to music may be in doubt, but their devotion to Spurs never has been. The duo have released four Spurs singles.

3. Neil Pearson Actor, Shelf stalwart and regular away traveller.

4. Charlie Whelan Spin doctor turned radio presenter. Fan kudos sealed when he cited John Pratt's 1978 screamer against Notts County as his favourite goal.

5. Peter Cook Loved Spurs a lot more than his comedy sidekick Dud.

6. Lemar Fame Academy winner and soul singer. A locally born Spur. Credit is due for his song *What If*, which includes the lines "Jumped into my ride, to avoid the lights, girl I took a different way, corner of White Hart Lane you were passing by."

7. Richard Littlejohn Professional controversialist. Genuine fan who gets to the Lane whenever he can.

8. Clare Tomlinson Sky Sports presenter and former Gooner press officer.

9. Bob Marley The reggae legend and Spurs fan died of cancer in 1981 at 36, three days before the replayed FA Cup final which saw Spurs beat Manchester City.

10. Norman Jay OBE DJ and Shelf-side regular.

11. Jude Law Hollywood actor. Fan despite growing up in Charlton country.

...AND THE ONES WE DON'T MENTION

For reasons all too clear

1. Bobby Davro 'Comedian'. Recently did an embarrassing pre-game interview on the pitch with Brian Alexander.

2. Iain Duncan Smith Former Tory leader. Dubbed himself 'The Quiet Man', which is doubtless why he sits in the Paxton.

3. Anthony from Blue Pop star.

4. Jodi Marsh Glamour girl.

5. Phil Collins Pop star.

6. Bruce Forsyth Entertainer and game-show host.

7. Status Quo Rock band.

8. Emma 'Baby Spice' Bunton Pop singer.

9. Antony Worrall Thompson Squeaky-voiced TV chef.

10. Rachel Stevens Formerly of S Club 7.

11. Darren Day 'Entertainer'.

CELLULOID, SITCOMS AND STAGE

Filling the match-day void

1. Those Glory Glory Days
The Channel 4 film, with screenplay by Spurs nut Julie Welch, was part of the First Love series. It helps fill the gap for those too young to have lived through the heady days of the early 1960s. It's the misty-eyed story of a young girl in thrall to Danny Blanchflower and the Double side: a chance to wallow in the romance of it all.

2. The Apprentice
An opportunity to see why Spurs fans objected to having Mr Alan Sugar in charge.

Sugar laid down a few rules in the first episode of the show: "I don't like liars. I don't like cheats. I don't like bullshitters. I don't like schmoozers. I don't like arse-lickers." Contestants were divided into two teams who carried out a series of business tasks. Afterwards, Sugar told the most pathetic contestant "You're fired". Episode six saw contestants promoting a mobile phone service to fans of Spurs, where Sugar still holds a 13 per cent stake.

3. Valiant

Gerry Francis acted as a consultant for this 2005 animated film about war-time carrier pigeons, advising on how pigeons move, eat, sleep and on details such as feather texture. The pigeon-fancier extraordinaire, who has a £40,000 pigeon loft at his home, says: "It's been great to tell the story of what courageous creatures they are. There's a medal given to brave animals, the Dickin Medal. Out of 61 that have been issued, pigeons have won 32. The lives they've saved, the people they've touched – it is hard to comprehend."

4. An Evening with Gary Lineker

The comic play by Arthur Smith and Chris England, originally staged to coincide with Italia 90, has little to do with football and a lot to do with sex – the former Spurs goalscoring paragon being the object of the fantasies of Monica, boringly married to Bill. It follows the adulterous shenanigans of the couple and their friends.

5. Harry Enfield and Chums

Paul Whitehouse wears a Spurs shirt as Cockney wideboy Lee.

6. Porridge

Fletch, who hails from Muswell Hill, wangles a weekend out of the clink, dividing his time between eating his loving missus's cooking and going down the Lane.

7. 2 Point 4 Children

The father of the 2.4 children, Gary, played by the late Gary Olsen, was, like the actor, a Spurs fan.

8. Auf Wiedersehen, Pet

Gary Olsen, who played Wayne Norris, the carpenter from Tilbury, was a Spurs fan.

9. David Ginola part 1

After hair-flicking and smouldering in the L'Oréal and Carte Noire adverts, Ginola attended the Royal Academy of Dramatic Arts. Gin's stage debut was alongside Bobby Davro in *Over The Rainbow* at the Cliffs Pavilion Theatre in Southend.

10. David Ginola part 2

We still await a Ginola cameo in *Holby City* after a planned appearance was shelved because of a clash with the Ginola family's pre-booked holiday. Ginola was due to play French surgeon Philippe Lestocquoy in an episode where a patient required an operation that could only be carried out in Paris.

11. David Ginola part 3

Ginola's first film, *The Last Drop*, centres on a unit of men dropped behind enemy lines in the midst of Operation Market Garden in World War 2. They are charged with spiriting a Nazi gold stash from a heavily guarded safe. As if this were not dicey enough, three renegade German soldiers are intent on plundering the same loot.

CEREBRAL SPURS

11 players who were more than just students of the game

1. Danny Blanchflower right-half, 1954-64

Danny Blanchflower could have instructed Wilde on the art of the epigram and taught Keats a thing or two about romantic poetry. He treated football like a PhD he was working on, horrifying managers by conducting experiments on the pitch. Naturally, he wrote his own autobiography and forthright newspaper columns (much to the alarm of the *Sunday Express* lawyers). In the RAF he won a scholarship to St Andrews University to study Maths, Physics and Applied Kinematics. While playing for Barnsley he studied for a BSc in economics. At Aston Villa, the vice-president helped train him in accountancy. Which is probably why the Spurs board decided he was too dangerous to manage the club and employed Terry Neill instead.

2. Jürgen Klinsmann striker, 1994/95, 1997/98

Klinsmann studied at the University of Life. Seriously. He regrets football prevented him from gaining his Arbitur, the German pre-university qualification, but says: "I learnt everything on the street." 'Everything' being English, French and Italian (he also speaks Schwabian, his local dialect, as well as German), the ability to negotiate his own contracts and a keen interest in world culture. Before internationals he sometimes sang a counter-cultural hymn from the 1960s, *Alle Menschen Werden Bruder (All People Will Be Brothers)*, instead of the German anthem.

3. Vivien Woodward centre-forward/inside-forward, 1901-09

An amateur throughout his career, Woodward worked as an architect. He was a Spurs director as well as a player, and his team-mates called him Sir.

4. Tony Galvin winger, 1978-87
Tony Galvin the footballer was pretty one-dimensional; Tony Galvin the man had onion layers. Well, he had a BA Hons degree in Russian from Hull University.

5. John Lacy centre-back, 1978-83
Being an economics graduate, Lacy was a good learner. Which was lucky, as the gangly defender had plenty still to learn when he arrived at White Hart Lane.

6. Gudni Bergsson utility man, 1988-95
The Icelandic utility man was a law student before joining Spurs.

7. Garth Crooks striker, 1980-85
Football wasn't enough for Crooks. There was *Top of the Pops* to present, social sciences to study, a mind to expand. He recalls a kind of reverse nirvana during his studies at Tottenham Tech when he realised he wasn't the kingpin, but a pawn at the bottom of a management structure. You can have all the education in the world but still not realise your shorts are too tight or you speak as if reading from an autocue.

8. Cecil Poynton full-back, 1922-33
Poynton studied physiotherapy in the 1940s… and became club physio in 1972. He once boasted to left-back Tony Want that the electric pad he was using on his leg "could kill a tank of goldfish".

9. George Robb winger, 1951-58
The former schoolteacher learned a salutary lesson in new-age football when he won his first and last England cap in the famous 6-3 defeat to Hungary in 1953. When a knee injury ended his career, Robb went back to school.

10. Les Allen centre-forward, 1959-65
Quite the sporting all-rounder, Les Allen was a little late making the grade as a footballer and in the meantime trained as an architect.

11. Ralph Coates winger, 1971-78
Coates took a psychology course in the 1990s and is convinced it's the way forward for football. "If you can, get the players together and ask why the dressing room is white," he says. "Would they prefer green or pink? See what the majority of the players want to make them happy."

CLASSIC CHANTS

All together now...

1. Glory Glory (and all its variations)
To the tune of *John Brown's Body*. Its first incarnation – the one that rang out around the ground on those 1960s European glory nights – ran simply:
Glory glory hallelujah
Glory glory hallelujah
Glory glory hallelujah
As the Spurs go marching on
Spurs now play a longer and more involved version at White Hart Lane after a win, which is scarcely ever sung.

2. It's A Grand Old Team
Gets frequent outings, but invariably tails off after your heart goes who-oh-oh-oh…
It's a grand old team to play for
It's a grand old team to see
And if you know your history
It's enough to make your heart go
Who-oh-oh-oh
We don't care what the other team say
What the hell do we care?
Cos we only know that there's gonna be a show
And that Tottenham Hotspur will be there

> CECIL POYNTON BOASTED THAT THE ELECTRIC PAD HE WAS USING "COULD KILL A TANK OF GOLDFISH"

3. MacNamara's Band
A classic from the 1950s (when it was sung by The Evergreens), *MacNamara's Band* is played before games and sometimes whips up a bit of clapping but has otherwise been put out to pasture.
Oh the whistle blows
The cockerel crows
And now we're in the game
It's up to you, you Lilywhites
To play the Tottenham way
Oh, there's other teams
In other towns
Some big and some are small
But then they see at White Hart Lane
The greatest of them all
La la la laaa, la la la laa laaa, la la la la la la la la laaaa….

4. We Are Tottenham

To the tune of Rod Stewart's *We Are Sailing*. A current, if uninventive, favourite.

We are Tott'nam, we are Tott'nam
Super Tott'nam from the Lane
We are Tott'nam, we are Tott'nam
We are Tott'nam from the Lane

5. Tell Me Mum

To the tune of *Que Sera Sera*. From 1991.

Tell me mum, me mum
To put the champagne on ice
We're going to Wembley twice
Tell me mum, me mum

6. Blue And White Army

Usually sung with the current manager's name at the front, this old favourite had to be doctored to deny the uncomfortable truth during the George Graham era.

Bloke in the raincoat's blue and white army!

7. Sing, Sing Wherever You May Be

To the tune of *Lord Of The Dance*. Sung during 1981/82 when Spurs were initially up for the Quadruple, but still optimistic about the Treble after defeat to Liverpool in the League Cup final.

Sing, sing, wherever you may be
We lost the League Cup at Wem-ber-lee
But we'll be back to win the other three
And we'll go down in history

A 1991 variation followed with the crucial couplet:

We beat the scum at Wem-ber-lee
They got one and we got three

8. When The Spurs Go Marching In

To the tune of *When The Saints Go Marching In*. Starting slowly, eventually speeding up and developing refrains, this can make the hairs stand on the back of your neck, but more often collapses into an unholy mess.

Oh when the Spurs
Go marching in
Oh when the Spurs go marching in
I want to be in that number
When the Spurs go marching in

9. We're So Broke It's Unbelievable
Sung at the 1991 FA Cup final.

10. We're The Shelf Side
Shelf side/Park Lane end repartee:
We're the Shelf side, we're the Shelf side
We're the Shelf side, Tottenham!
We're the Park Lane, we're the Park Lane
We're the Park Lane, Tottenham!
…Descending into mutually adoring cries of "Yiddos! Yiddos!" Theoretically the Paxton can join in too, but they tend not to bother, prompting "Paxton, Paxton, give us a song!" Also good for proclaiming your identity at away games.

11. Ossie's Dream (from 1981)
The opening verse is still a regular:
(Come on you) Spurs are on their way to Wembley*
Tottenham's gonna do it again
They can't stop 'em, the boys from Tottenham
The boys from White Hart Lane
*replace with Cardiff where applicable

CLASSIC DERBIES
Losing is not an option

1. Spurs 3 Arsenal 1 First ever Wembley FA Cup semi-final, 14 April 1991
Spurs in danger of going out of existence, Arsenal in danger of doing the Double and Gazza virtually rushed from the operating theatre to the Wembley pitch: Spurs achieved the impossible and how. Gazza's scorching 35-yard free kick, two from Lineker and just an Alan Smith effort from the Gooners.

2. Spurs 5 Chelsea 1 League Cup semi-final, second leg, 23 January 2002
What a way to break a 12-year hoodoo. Iversen, Sherwood, Sheringham, Davies and Rebrov got the goals, but the whole team played a blinder.

3. Spurs 5 Arsenal 0 4 April 1983
Braces from Chris Hughton and Mark Falco and one from Alan Brazil. Hearty revenge for a 2-0 loss at the Library. We finished fourth and they finished a satisfying six places and 11 points below us.

4. Arsenal 4 Spurs 4 22 February 1958
A Ron Henry own goal set Arsenal on their way, and Spurs had to score twice in the last four minutes to earn a point. Two goals from Tommy Harmer, two from Bobby Smith, while Cliff Jones had a hand in three of them on his debut.

5. Spurs 4 Arsenal 3 26 August 1961
Terry Dyson became the only player to score a league hat-trick against the Gooners.

6. Arsenal 4 Spurs 4 15 October 1963
No Spurs player has scored more goals against the Arse than Bobby Smith – nine in total – and his brace at Highbury helped to earn a point in a high-scoring derby in front of 68,000 fans. Under Billy Wright, Arsenal weren't boring but they weren't very good either.

7. Spurs 4 Arsenal 4 6 October 1962
Three-nil up with goals from Mackay, White and Jones after 30 minutes, Spurs were clawed back to 3-2 by half-time. Blanchflower, White and Allen combined to set up Jones for a fourth but John MacLeod and Geoff String squared it up for the Gooners.

8. Spurs 4 Arsenal 5 13 November 2004
The highest aggregate score ever between the two sides, with nine different scorers. So we lost, but we spent most of the game putting the wind up them, and they spent most of it looking over their shoulders. And it was insanely exciting.

9. Spurs 5 West Ham 3 5 November 1927
Five goals in the first 25 minutes gave Spurs a 3-2 lead and they eventually humbled the Hammers 5-3. The highlight of a season when Spurs were relegated.

10. West Ham 2 Spurs 3 FA Cup quarter-final, 11 March 2001
What a corker. All Spurs in the first half, a Hammers onslaught in the second, with Neil Sullivan man of the match. The Spurs scorers were, of all people, Sergei Rebrov (two) and Gary Doherty. The Football Genius clambered into the crowd to celebrate afterwards and the win handed Spurs a semi-final tie with Arsenal.

11. Spurs 2 Arsenal 1 7 November 1999
Two up in 20 minutes courtesy of Iversen and Sherwood, followed by some demon defending, but most delightful of all, two Gooners sent for early baths.

CLASSIC GAMES
The ones that left us physically and mentally drained

1. Spurs 5 Atletico Madrid 1 Cup Winners' Cup final, Rotterdam, 15 May 1963
It started in Glasgow, continued via snow, ice and punch-ups in Eastern Europe and finished with Terry Dyson sipping champagne out of the Cup Winners' Cup in Rotterdam and Dave Mackay doing the twist. Jimmy Greaves called it "the greatest game I ever played in". In the dressing room before the game, Bill Nick ran through the Atletico Madrid team. Atletico were the holders. They were superhuman. Or so it seemed from Bill Nick's team talk. Danny Blanchflower leapt to his feet. "Hang on a minute boss. What's all this?" He began to rouse the team: "If their centre-half is big and ugly, then ours is bigger and uglier. No disrespect, Mo." Perhaps it was this speech that stirred Terry Dyson. The lesser light of the Double team, Dyson put on such a display that Bobby Smith told him afterwards to retire. From the off it was all Spurs. A Cliff Jones cross, a Jimmy Greaves half-volley – 1-0 after 15 minutes. For 20 minutes Spurs pummelled Atletico. Dyson rescued a lost ball, sent it across the box to John White who slotted home from 20 yards. After half-time, Atletico came alive. Ron Henry handled; Collar scored Atletico's penalty. Atletico attacked again and again, Spurs defended stoutly: Bill Brown was unbeatable. Then Dyson skinned Rivilia at right-back, floated in a cross and Madinabeytia fumbled into his own net. Atletico were sunk; Spurs were untouchable. Dyson set up Greaves for number four, then hurtled through the middle and scored number five from 25 yards. Dave Mackay, who was injured and out of the game, was seen to cry. Later he danced with the best of them, and The Beatles' *Please Please Me* still reminds him of that night.

2. Spurs 2 Benfica 1 European Cup semi-final, second leg, White Hart Lane, 5 April 1962
"A bit of bad luck around the penalty area." That's Bill Nick-speak for "monstrous injustice". Spurs had gone to Lisbon and played the Benfica of Eusébio, Coluna, Aguas and Germano. They scored three goals but the referee gave only one. Jimmy Greaves was given offside, but is convinced he wasn't. Bobby Smith was flagged up, yet the ball had passed two defenders on its way to goal. Benfica won 3-1, but there'd been away deficits before; Spurs had simply taken the opposition back to White Hart Lane and scored lots of goals. But this time Benfica scored – a stunner from Aguas after just 15 minutes. Spurs needed three. A curling John White cross cut out two defenders, Bobby Smith volleyed into Greaves's path and he slotted it home. The referee gave it but the linesman's flag was waving again; the third goal of the tie disallowed. The home attack mounted relentlessly. Another pass from John White found Bobby Smith. He killed it and cannoned it into the net. Four minutes into the second half, Cruz took White's legs. Penalty. Blanchflower dispatched it

nervelessly. One more to force the replay. Germano's hand batted away a Mackay header. Nothing given. John White played in Bobby Smith, but his shot hit the post. Many called it the best game ever seen at White Hart Lane, but Spurs had lost it.

3. Spurs 3 Manchester City 2 FA Cup final, Wembley, 14 May 1981
Ricky Villa sat crying in the Wembley dressing room. Neither he nor Spurs had played well – perhaps lucky to force a replay – and the eyes of Argentina had been on Villa. "Lift your head up – you're playing on Thursday," said Keith Burkinshaw. Burkinshaw is not sure why he decided to play the sometimes brilliant, often unreliable Villa. A Spurs fan would call it divine inspiration. The 100th FA Cup final take two was as glorious as take one had been dull. Villa scored, McKenzie got a glorious equaliser, but Spurs ran the first-half. The second began with a Manchester City penalty after Dave Bennett tumbled between Paul Miller and Chris Hughton. Twenty minutes passed. Hoddle chipped, Archibald turned, and Garth Crooks toe-poked: 2-2. Just as extra time loomed once more, Ricky Villa swerved, shimmied and dummied and scored *that* goal.

4. Spurs 4 Feyenoord 2 UEFA Cup second round, first leg, White Hart Lane, 19 October 1983
Not a classic game, but a classic 45 minutes. Forty-five minutes of Spurs' finest, purest football ever. Hoddle shared a pitch with a veteran Johan Cruyff and a young Ruud Gullit and showed them both how to play. It was perhaps his greatest performance, as he flighted exquisite balls from midfield. Many of them were hit behind the Feyenoord full-back, where Tony Galvin charged on to them to great effect. Three perfect Hoddle passes set up goals one, two and four for Archibald, Galvin and Galvin again. Not even a traditional collapse in the second-half could take away the shine. Spurs won 2-0 in Rotterdam and at White Hart Lane in May they lifted the cup.

5. Spurs 4 Leeds United 2 White Hart Lane, 28 April 1975
Cup wins, glory games and derbies – few can match the atmosphere of the night Spurs weren't relegated. Nearly 50,000 came – what if this was goodbye? And surely it was: there'd been defeat to Chelsea, defeat to Arsenal. And now it was Leeds. The brief: to win the last game of the season against the champions to stay up. They did it, and Cyril Knowles was the star. Reaney took down Alfie Conn just outside the area and Knowles curled a peach of a free kick into the top corner. Next he scored a penalty (2-0), then set up Martin

> HODDLE SHARED A PITCH WITH CRUYFF AND A YOUNG GULLIT AND SHOWED THEM BOTH HOW TO PLAY

Chivers (3-0). Leeds replied, but Alfie Conn dribbled past three men for a fourth. A second strike from Leeds did nothing to dull the jubilation.

6. Nottingham Forest 0 Spurs 3 15 November 1980

As a matter of course, Brian Clough never spoke to Keith Burkinshaw after games. But this time, he collared him to say: "That was absolutely fantastic. You gave us a real hammering there." Ardiles scored and Archibald got two, but all over the park, Spurs players excelled. The midfield trio of Hoddle, Ardiles and Villa were superb. Says Burkinshaw, "It was probably the best ever performance by that team."

7. Spurs 2 Liverpool 1 FA Cup quarter-final, Anfield, 12 March 1995

The year Sugar and Venables collided, the year they tried to ban Spurs from the FA Cup, the year Ossie attempted hara-kiri, the year of Klinsmann. Only in years such as those can Spurs win at Anfield. Only with a player such as Klinsmann in the side could they do it in such style. Gerry Francis was now in charge, and Spurs had been shored up, but Mark Walters still left the defence for dead, setting up Robbie Fowler to score. Which Spurs was playing today? Gutsy Spurs or folding Spurs? David Howells stood firm in midfield, and as the first-half fizzled out, Spurs scored. Klinsmann knocked down for Sheringham, and he flighted it beautifully into the far right corner. The second half drew on. Winning a replay would be triumph enough. Then Sheringham flicked on and Klinsmann placed it in the right-hand corner. Anfield applauded Spurs and an emotional Klinsmann off the pitch.

8. AC Milan 1 Spurs 1 UEFA Cup semi-final, second leg, San Siro, 19 April 1972

Spurs had won the home leg 2-1, but the Milan of Gianni Rivera had scored an away goal. A famous Italian 1-0 home win was now all that was required. For the first five minutes Spurs floundered. Then the ball dropped to Steve Perryman. He had scored two long-range scorchers in the first leg, so the defence quickly converged. But Perryman squared the ball into the path of captain Alan Mullery whose first-time shot curved and soared, unstoppable. The Spurs midfield contained Milan, while full-backs Joe Kinnear and Cyril Knowles overlapped and caused havoc. Rivera scored a penalty in the second half and Milan came again, but Spurs stood firm. They had reached their first European final since Atletico Madrid in 1963.

9. Spurs 10 Everton 4 White Hart Lane, 11 October 1958

Bill Nick's first game had the air of a calling card, a token of what was to come. The supremely skillful Tommy Harmer, whom Bill Nick had recalled, scored the third, and the story goes he set up the other nine. John Ryden, Terry Medwin and George Robb were all on the scoresheet, Alfie Stokes got two, while Bobby Smith scored four. "Can't promise this every week, boss," Smith told Nicholson afterwards.

10. Spurs 7 Newcastle United 0 White Hart Lane, 18 November 1950
Newcastle had Jackie Milburn, Joe Harvey and George Robledo; Spurs were without Ron Burgess. Spurs had been a First Division team for just three months. But Newcastle were taken apart. Eddie Bailey and Les Medley were their scourges – Medley scored a hat-trick. At the other end Ted Ditchburn became bored with standing in an unthreatened goal. Alf Ramsey, Les Bennett and Charlie Walters were the other scorers in the last of an eight-game winning run.

11. Derby County 0 Spurs 3 County Ground, 8 December 1990
Gazza's official cliché was that he turned matches. But he did much more than that for Spurs: he carried the team to an FA Cup final. This game showcased his Atlas-like abilities in microcosm. He scored a breathtaking hat-trick and won the applause of the Derby fans. One Spurs fan who found himself in their end was patted on the back and congratulated. Gazza's display, said the Derby fans, was worth the defeat.

CLASSIC KITS

Kits of good karma

1. 1970s home shirt Round neck, cockerel on ball, plain white, no fuss. Lovely. Bill Nick said how much he liked this one when his wife Darkie came home wearing a retro version from the Spurs store. If it was good enough for Bill Nick…

2. 1960/61 Double shirt Plain white, v-neck, shield with a cockerel in it (no ball).

3. All white, the cup kit What was it about the all-white kit that made the glory glory nights that bit more glorious (especially against Dukla Prague in the snow)?

4. 1980/81, 1981/82 home kit (Le Coq Sportif) V-neck, unfussy trimmings (a narrow navy band around the neck, ends of the sleeves and top of the shorts). The kit of Hod, Ossie, Ricky and two FA Cups. And what more appropriate kit manufacturer than one whose logo let us wear two cockerels on our shirts?

5. 2004/05 home shirt (Kappa) The red on the front is problematic but classiest in a long time. Better quality than the bobble-fests of the previous couple of seasons.

6. 2004/05 third kit (Kappa) The home kit in negative. Perfect.

7. 2004/05 away goalkeeping kit (Kappa) Goalkeepers in all green. You can't beat it. The pale blue home goalkeeper's kit was hard to fault, too.

8. 1994/95 away shirt (Umbro) Purply/dark blue affair. Jürgen looked smashing in it when he scored his debut goal against Sheffield Wednesday. Huge badge though.

9. 1986-89 home shirt (Hummel) The 1987 FA Cup final shirt. Minimal navy piping, a collar-and-v combination neck with a bit of navy to it, white band round the waist of the shorts. Dodgy zig-zag pattern but you can't beat a Holsten shirt.

10. 1989-91 home shirt (Hummel) The kit that took Spurs to the FA Cup final. A bit of navy piping, a navy band round the neck and a lozenge in the centre of the band with THFC written in it. Let down by pointless arrows on the sleeves and shorts.

11. 1946-59 Ted Ditchburn's jersey Ditchburn wore a range of woolly roll-neck jumpers with various degrees of ribbing to them. Sleekest has to be from 1952/53, a close-fitting number with ribbing at the cuffs and in a v-shape around the neck.

CLASSIC PLAYER CHANTS

Worthy of the Bard himself

1. Nice one Cyril
Nice one son
Nice one Cyril!
Let's have another one

2. We've got the G men
In Greaves and Gilzean
They are the world's best
Goal-scoring machine
So we say
C'mon Tottenham
Score a goal or two
Or three or four or more
For the fans of Britain's best team

3. My name is Nicola Berti
I'm aged around 30
I come from the best team in town – Inter!
When I walk down the street
All the people I meet

They say, hey, gorgeous! What's your name?
My name is Nicola Berti…

Along similar lines:
My name is Jose Dominguez
I play on the wingez
I play for the best team around – Tott'nam!
When I walk down the street
All the people I meet
They say, hey, wee man! What's your name?
I say my name's Jose Dominguez…

4. Steffen Freund's a football genius!

5. All the runs that Ronny does are winding
To the tune of Oasis's *Wonderwall*
And all the goals that Ronny scores are blinding
There are many things that I would like to say to you
But I don't know how
But maybe, you're gonna be the one that saves me
And after all, you're my Rosenthal

6. Three fat Gooners standing in a wall
To *Ten Green Bottles* after Gazza's free kick in the 1991 FA Cup semi-final
Three fat Gooners standing in a wall
And if one Paul Gascoigne should bend it round the wall
There'll be one sick Seaman standing in the goal

7. All things bright and beautiful
All creatures great and small
All things wise and wonderful
We call them Frankie Saul

8. La la la and Jennings is better than Yashin

9. Gilzean, Gilzean, Gilzean, Gilzean, Gilzean
To the tune of *The First Noel*
Born is the king of White Hart Lane

10. Sha la la la Mullery

11. Who's got a lovely wife?

To the tune of *Knees Up Mother Brown*. Sung of Jamie Redknapp and Louise, and earlier also about Ian Walker and his model wife Susie.

Who's got a lovely wife?
Jamie Redknapp, Jamie Redknapp
Who's got a lovely wife?

CLASSIC QUOTES

11 great rebuffs and rebuttals

1. Cliff Jones: *"You're giving me a pat on the back are you, Bill? That's unusual."*
Bill Nicholson: *"Yes, but remember, a pat on the back is only three foot away from a kick up the arse."*

2. *"Numbers are a thing with me. I have this thing about four. I don't know why four. My favourite used to be five and then seven. Then I got into this thing about 13 because nothing would be done in fours and nine and four are 13. I don't know where the nine comes from. I got it into my head because nine and four makes 13. That's like six and seven. I can't bear to see them together because that's 13 again. So when I go out onto the park I won't go out sixth or seventh. I'll either be fifth or eighth."* Gazza's logic.

3. Reporter: *"Is Klinsmann Spurs' biggest-ever signing?"*
Ossie Ardiles: *"No, I was."*

4. *"There used to be a football club over there."* Keith Burkinshaw on resigning in 1984 as Irving Scholar transformed the club into a 'leisure group'.

5. *"Is there a diving school in London?"* Jürgen Klinsmann on signing for Spurs.

6. *"The silly bastard only tried to save it, didn't he?"* Gazza to Terry Venables after his free kick sailed past David Seaman in the 1991 FA Cup semi-final.

7. *"I rugby-tackled him once. He then gave me three dummies on the trot."* Watford defender Darren Bazeley on Ginola.

8. *"If I had to pick someone to tiptoe through my bed of tulips, this is the man I'd pick."* BBC Radio's Maurice Edelston, on Martin Chivers.

9. *"It's better to fail aiming high, than to succeed aiming low."* Bill Nicholson.

10. *"An after-dinner speech is an odd thing. You eat a meal you don't want so you can get up and tell a load of stories you can't remember to people who have already heard them. My father gave me the best advice on after-dinner speaking. Be sincere. Be brief. Be seated. That in mind, ladies and gentlemen, I give you the FA Cup."*
Bill Nicholson, 20 May 1967.

11. *"The great fallacy is that the game is first and last about winning. It's nothing of the kind. The game is about glory. It's about doing things in style, with a flourish, about going out and beating the other lot, not waiting for them to die of boredom."*
Danny Blanchflower.

CLUB RECORD SALES

Keeping the accountant happy

Fee	Player	To	Date
£5.5m	Paul Gascoigne	Lazio	May 1992
£5.25m	Nick Barmby	Middlesbrough	May 1995
£5m	Helder Postiga	Porto	July 2004
£4.25m	Chris Waddle	Marseille	May 1989
£3.5m	Teddy Sheringham	Manchester Utd	June 1997
£3m	Luke Young	Charlton Athletic	July 2001
£3m	David Ginola	Aston Villa	July 2000
£2.5m	Ian Walker	Leicester City	July 2001
£2.5m	Neil Ruddock	Liverpool	August 1993
£2.3m	Paul Stewart	Liverpool	July 1992
£2.25m	Allan Nielsen	Watford	July 2000

CLUB RECORD SIGNINGS

...or giving him nightmares

Fee	Player	From	Date
£11m	Sergei Rebrov	Dynamo Kiev	May 2000
£8.1m	Dean Richards	Southampton	September 2001
£7m	Robbie Keane	Leeds United	August 2002
£7m	Jermain Defoe	West Ham	February 2004
£6.25m	Helder Postiga	Porto	June 2003

£6m	Les Ferdinand	Newcastle United	August 1997
£5m	Ben Thatcher	Wimbledon	July 2000
£4.5m	Chris Armstrong	Crystal Palace	June 1995
£4.2m	Ruel Fox	Newcastle United	October 1995
£4m	Chris Perry	Wimbledon	July 1999
£4m	Tim Sherwood	Blackburn Rovers	February 1999

CRAP KITS

Call the fashion police

1. 1890-96 home kit Red and navy colours, so perhaps not surprisingly Spurs were known as the 'Tottenham Reds'. The indignity…

2. 1896-98 home kit Spurs decided on a change of colours to mark their step up to the Southern League. Unfortunately they chose chocolate and gold.

3. 1991-93 goalkeeper shirt (Umbro) The Viking's outfit came in dark blue or bright yellow, had quilted shoulders and was decorated with multi-coloured streaks.

4. 1979/80 away kit (Admiral) Pale yellow with huge navy collar and v-neck. The border of the v-neck featured repeated Admiral logos. Two navy panels descended from the shoulders, one containing a large white cockerel and ball, while a big white Admiral logo was squidged in next to the other.

5. 1991-93 away shirt (Umbro) Bright yellow shirt spanned the Lineker-Sheringham transition. It had a pale blue and chequered navy blue flash on the right shoulder and left shorts leg, a yellow band in the navy collar and a nasty Umbro-and-stripes pattern in the fabric.

6. 1993-95 away kit (Umbro) Another season, another tasteless kit. This one had the same pattern in the fabric, but was sky blue with wide-spaced navy pinstripes. Just above the 'Holsten' was a pin-stripe pattern with much narrower spacing that spelt SPURS across the upper chest.

7. 1985-87 home kit (Hummel) More tasteful but scarily 1980s variation of the 1993–95 Umbro away kit. There was an arrow pattern down either side of the shorts, along the sleeves and across the chest just above the Holsten logo. Diagonal pin stripes rose from the arrows to meet the navy piping on the shoulders.

8. 1995-97 home shirt (Pony) A nasty creation comprising a press studs-and-collar neck, material with a Pony logo pattern, a weird-shaped shield badge and shorts with white stripes and a zig-zag pattern down the sides.

9. 2002-04 goalkeeping kit (Kappa) Quite tasteful but Kasey Keller's insistence on wearing a shirt two sizes too small made him look like the Riddler.

10. 1950/51 home kit The cockerel was a strange stubby cartoon-like creature with a tail reminiscent of a peacock's. But at least we won the league in it.

11. 1991-93 home kit Worn for the 1991 FA Cup final, this outfit comprised a perfectly acceptable shirt matched with daft baggy shorts with white semi-circles on the outside of each leg "as though their shirts were hanging out of the bottom of their knickers," as my mum put it.

CULT HEROES

11 ways to achieve cult status

1. Cyril Knowles

It started with the lad in the Hovis ad heaving his bicycle up a Yorkshire hill, taking Grandad his Hovis loaf, to be greeted with: "Nice one, Cyril!" Soon, any Knowles pass, shimmy or run met with the same cry from the terraces. When the Cockerel Chorus added some extra lyrics, gave it a cheesy tune and had a 1973 chart hit with it, a cult phenomenon was born. Knowles was always grinning and the crowd grinned with him. The two goals that saved Spurs from relegation in 1975 sealed his status.

2. Steffen Freund

He couldn't pass or shoot. What was Steffen Freund good for, wondered the fans. The answer was soon clear: ball-winning. When Freund wasn't there, the defence looked as naked as the day it was born. With ball-winning came commitment. He tackled Roy Keane and comically fled to escape the consequences. He waved the crowd on, demanding more noise. And, crucially for his cult status, he just couldn't score. "Shoooooot!" implored the crowd when the ball dropped to him anywhere forward of the centre-circle. Freund inevitably responded with a well-placed ball into the upper tier. Eventually, Spurs fans simply referred to him as 'The Football Genius', the artist formerly known as Freund. Some fans say he hijacked Teddy Sheringham's farewell match, which was also his own. Maybe so, but when he took off his shirt to reveal a T-shirt with "Thank you!" scrawled on it, you had to love him.

3. Paul Robinson

We could tell straightaway he was good. Then he ran around like a loon taking every free kick in our half when we were chasing the game against Charlton in November 2004. Throwing his gloves into the crowd bumped up the cult volume. Then Robbo became "England, England's number one" and there were waves, hand-claps and thumbs-up every time he heard his chant. Just before the second-half began against Manchester City at the Lane in March, Robbo booted the ball into the crowd. The crowd gave it back. Robbo returned it again and again, before the referee spoiled the fun, forcing us to watch the second-half of a very dull match.

4. Ronny Rosenthal

When Ronny Rosenthal came to Spurs the abiding image was of him missing the greatest sitter of all time while playing for Liverpool. Rocket Ronny did nothing at Spurs to banish the memory, but often revived flagging games by coming on as sub and repeatedly charging headlong to the opposition goal line before losing the ball. There was already a touch of the cult about his super-fast madcap runs, but Rocket turned cult superhero in the space of an evening. With Spurs 2-0 down in an FA Cup replay at Southampton, Rocket came off the bench just before half-time and scored the most stunning hat-trick, firing Spurs to a 6-2 win.

5. Erik Thorstvedt

When times at Tottenham were gloomy, big Erik the Viking was a splash of colour. After the terrible televised clanger on his debut, he fought on. After his first clean sheet came at Southampton, he hurled his gloves into the crowd. It was the beginning of a beautiful friendship.

6. Graham Roberts

Nothing could secure cult status faster than booting Charlie Nicholas into the stand, as Roberts once did. On top of that he was well 'ard, liked to score with pounding long-range shots, and bagged the equaliser against Anderlecht in the 1984 UEFA Cup final second leg, which ultimately led to the successful penalty shoot-out.

7. Phil Beal

Phil Beal was like an old armchair, always there to provide comfort in times of trouble. With Beal at the back, nothing could go wrong. For cultability, see the one and only goal of his career, at home to QPR in 1969. He found the ball deep in Spurs' territory, took off on an epic run, completed a neat one-two with Jimmy Greaves, before unleashing an unstoppable bullet.

8. Alfie Conn

So much hair and so much skill. Alfie Conn was irresistible. In his early appearances as substitute the crowd was tantalised. On his full debut he scored a hat-trick against Newcastle. Inconsistency was part of the package. Where coaches found an unmanageable wild child, the crowd saw a free spirit. Conn provided one of Spurs' all-time cult moments when he sat on the ball against Leeds (see Absolute Best Moments). He liked to entertain and when Terry Neill suggested putting a lid on the wanderlust Conn didn't respond well. After just 38 games, Bill Nick's last signing was packed off to his native Scotland to join Celtic, much to the fans' chagrin.

9. Willie Young

'Big Wullie' was a lumbering beast of a centre-back but began to win some love for his bruising, boisterous commitment. When Keith Burkinshaw replaced Terry Neill he was less keen, and Young followed Neill to Highbury.

10. Jimmy Pearce

To a select band of connoisseurs on the Shelf, Jimmy 'Champagne' Pearce was that rare vintage, a fine wine with a bit of fizz, a full-bodied, heady blend of clever flicks and touches. Ultimately immortalised by David Coleman's spare commentary of the Rapid Bucharest UEFA Cup demolition in 1971. "Pearce! Neat!"

11. Martin Jol

The first ever cult manager? Surely all the ingredients are there: he's got no hair and we don't care ("Why do they sing that song about my hair?" a vaguely hurt-looking Jol once asked a fan); he has a big Dutch face and a promising line in amusing quotes; and he has brothers called Dick and Cock. If proof is still needed, a chorus of "I love Martin Jol, Martin Jol loves me" is becoming familiar at the Lane.

> BLANCHFLOWER ON EGOTIST BOB LORD: "HE'S A SELF-MADE MAN WHO WORSHIPS HIS CREATOR"

DANNY BLANCHFLOWER: FOOTBALLER, WIT, POET…

Words to the wise

1. *"Winning isn't everything, but wanting to win is."*

2. *"He's a self-made man who worships his creator."* On Burnley chairman, president of the Football League and renowned egotist Bob Lord.

3. *"Stimulating. Every pass from Dick is an adventure."*
On playing alongside Dick Keith for Northern Ireland.

4. *"Thank you for your idea, Billy. I feel you would do well to remember that ideas are funny things. They never work unless you do."*
Responding to a suggestion from the work-shy Billy Campbell before a Northern Ireland game.

5. After a Northern Ireland game, a reporter asks Blanchflower for his opinion on George Best…
"George makes a greater appeal to the senses than Finney or Matthews did. His movements are quicker, lighter, more balletic. George offers grander surprises to the mind and the eye. He has ice in his veins, warmth in his heart and timing and balance in his feet."
Reporter: *"Yeah, yeah, but how do you rate George as a player, Danny?"*

6. *"If you can get today right, it makes yesterday a pleasant memory and tomorrow a vision of hope."*

7. *"A luxury? It's the bad players who are a luxury."*

8. *"We try to equalise before the other team have scored."*

9. *"In good or bad times there has always been a vitality at Tottenham which has absorbed me. A main road passes the front door and perhaps the vibrant flow of life so near stimulates the atmosphere and keeps the place alert and alive."*

10. *"A game of soccer is like a conversation: if your companions do not talk very much and you have no need or inspiration to say anything to them, the conversation dies."*

11. *"The business of captaincy demands a strong will, it has more headaches and heartaches, if it is cared for properly, than it has of glory."*

DEFECTIONS

After 123 years there's scarcely enough defectors to scrape a squad together. In order of villainy...

1. Sol Campbell: the story in quotes

13 May 2000, Alan Sugar: "We can break away from our pay structure in special cases like Campbell. Money shouldn't be an issue. We will do everything in our power to keep him. He'll be a Tottenham player next year unless he doesn't want to be."

4 August, Campbell: "My heart and soul is here and I want to play for Spurs."

20 November, George Graham: "It's all very well people saying that we could have sold him for £15m, but that will never happen if the player doesn't want to move until his contract ends. I can't understand him not sitting down and listening to our financial offer, even if he turns it down. He says he is Tottenham through and through. He should show a bit of courtesy by at least talking about a new contract."

17 December, Campbell: "Being a Spurs fan as a boy and a player for so many years, it would be hard to sign for Arsenal."

1 January 2001, Campbell: "I want to play for Tottenham. I am going nowhere. I've been here so long. For me to do well at this club means everything."

25 May, Spurs spokesman John Fennelley: "We made an offer last night and it's the best offer the club has ever made to a player."

14 June, Marc Overmars: "I'm really surprised Sol Campbell looks set to join Arsenal. I had a strong feeling he'd sign for my current team Barcelona. It's a shock he seems

to have chosen to cross the North London divide instead. It would have been great to see Sol put his skills to test in a new league."

19 June, Barça manager Carles Rexach: "We have had very positive discussions with Sol Campbell. I believe he will make a decision very soon and I hope it will be good news for Barcelona. We also have Champions League football."

29 June, Inter spokesman: "Talks between Inter and Sol Campbell are going very well. Sol Campbell is a superb player and we hope he will decide to come here."

1 July, Bayern Munich vice-president Karl-Heinz Rummenigge: "We were interested in Campbell three months back, but not any more. Such a signing would create problems in this club. He was too expensive. He wanted £5.8 million."

3 July, Campbell ignores Spurs' best-ever offer to sign for Arsenal on a Bosman free.

2. Terry Neill
"It is difficult to put into words the elation I felt at becoming Arsenal manager. It was just so nice to be back again." Granted, Neill suffered some rough treatment in his first months but telling the fans to "go and get stuffed" after the survival-clinching Leeds game just wasn't nice. Neill puts a plausible case for his departure from Spurs, and a semi-plausible one for joining Arsenal. But he was headed up Avenall Road just two weeks after quitting N17. It's just not cricket.

3. Herbert Chapman
The footballing fates got their wires crossed when Herbert Chapman came to Tottenham. He was an unremarkable inside-forward who played 71 games between 1904 and 1907. At Arsenal he was a managerial legend pioneering the WM formation that spread through Europe, taking dour, defensive football with it.

4. Willie Young
Popular with the fans for a time but ultimately he was a Terry Neill stooge and an altogether Goonerish player. Young was brawny and good in the air. That was it really. By 1976/77 Young's lack of skill was showing through and Keith Burkinshaw dropped him. He rejoined Neill at Highbury, where of course the Gooners loved him.

5. George Hunt
George Hunt, the much-loved 'Chesterfield Tough', signed for Spurs over Arsenal and became their highest scorer until Bobby Smith. But he found his first-team outings strangely limited under unpopular manager Jack Tresadern and moved to Arsenal.

6. Freddie Cox

Respect is due for the Distinguished Flying Cross Freddie won during World War 2, but what a shame he let himself down by signing for the Arsenal. Cox was a regular on the Spurs wing just after the war until he was ousted by Sonny Walters, whereupon he slunk away to Highbury for a fee of £12,000 in 1949.

7. Peter Kyle

A temperamental, waxed moustachioed, black-haired centre-forward, Kyle played 41 times for Spurs at the beginning of the 20th century. Defection was less serious since the Gunners had yet to invade north London. But it still seemed fitting that, when he left after being suspended over "a breach of the training rules", he should pop up at Woolwich Arsenal.

8. Ly Burrows

You can take the man out of the Gooners, but you can't take the Gooner out of the man. Arsenal were still a Woolwich team when the ferocious full-back was invited to play for Spurs in 1884. An amateur player, Burrows served Spurs until 1897 but snuck back to play ten Football League games for Arsenal while attached to Spurs.

9. Pat Jennings

"It was an opportunity to create the biggest embarrassment for whoever was responsible in the club for letting me go. I hope I did that. I was that angry." Consider: Jennings was at Spurs for 14 years; he was Players' Player of the Year the previous season; he was perhaps the best in the world; he was just 32. Burkinshaw hurried him out with the words: "The team are leaving for Sweden tomorrow and I don't want to take you because you'll be an embarrassment to Barry Daines." Jennings's treatment excuses the unforgiveable. "Playing against Tottenham was horrible, horrible," he says. He's now back at the Lane for every home game.

10. Jimmy Robertson

Bill Nick's one moment of madness. The fans' beloved leggy winger was shipped to Highbury in 1968 in exchange for David Jenkins, who proved scant consolation. Robertson was laudably mediocre in two seasons at Arsenal.

11. Peter McWilliam

After World War 1, the popular manager was producing flowing football with the Tottenham stamp on it and taking Spurs to new heights. He fell out with the board over failure to make funds available for new players. The whiff of discontent reached Middlesbrough, who tempted him up north. He had the grace to return when Spurs came crawling back in 1938, but did he really have to scout for Arsenal in between?

ECHOES OF GLORIES PAST: THE UEFA CUP

After the Double, Bill Nick dismantled and rebuilt his team. The Spurs side of the early 1970s came closest to recreating the glory days, with League Cup wins in 1971 and 1973, a UEFA Cup in 1972 and a UEFA Cup runners-up spot in 1974. But in the league, Spurs dropped from third, to sixth to eighth to 11th…

1. Pat Jennings, goalkeeper

In *The Glory Game*, Hunter Davies interviews a Leeds United scout sent to compile a dossier of weaknesses on Spurs before their FA Cup quarter-final. The scout reels off a list of fallibilities until he reaches Pat Jennings. "I take my bloody hat off to him," says the scout. "I've thought once or twice I've spotted his weakness. I saw him once go for the near post a bit early. I thought that's it, that's his weakness. But he never did it again. Every time I've seen him he's been magnificent." Strikers struck where and when Jennings wanted them to: in one-on-ones he was always in control. He beat out impossible balls with whichever part of his anatomy happened to be nearest. His angles were faultless. His distribution merely competent. Before games he was a chronic worrier, but during them he ruled his area calmly. "People just kept on putting me on another rung of the ladder and I managed to respond to it," says Jennings, reflecting on how he came to be the greatest keeper of his day.

2. Joe Kinnear, right-back

When Phil Beal broke his arm in 1967 it gave Joe Kinnear his chance. When Kinnear broke his leg in 1969, it let in Ray Evans. That was how it went for Kinnear at Spurs. There was no doubt he was good. Youngest on the pitch, he was man of the match in the 1967 FA Cup final. After he broke his leg he was boosted by rumours that Manchester United had made a £70,000 bid for him. He was a fast overlapper, a good passer and a sharp tackler. But Evans was good too and the right-back spot seesawed between the two. Kinnear asked Bill Nick for a transfer in 1972. Luckily for Kinnear it was turned down and he played in both legs of Spurs' 1972 UEFA Cup triumph. He was in the team for the 1971 League Cup win and again in 1973, but in 1975 he left for Brighton, his last playing stint before coaching and management.

3. Cyril Knowles, left-back

Cyril Knowles owed one of his finest hours to Romark, Terry Neill's hypnotist. Well, maybe. Before the game against reigning champions Leeds that Spurs had to win to stay up in 1975, Romark told Knowlesy he was a steel girder. He suspended him between the backs of two chairs, head to toe, and Pat Jennings sat on the middle of him. Romark told Knowlesy to remember the positive feelings he had the last time he played well and he told him he would score two goals. The next day Knowles tormented the Leeds defence during Spurs' 4-2 win and scored from a free kick and a penalty. A cool and strong-tackling full-back, Cyril Knowles was born to overlap. Knowles's storming runs and fine crosses were pure entertainment. A persistent knee injury forced him to retire in 1975; success followed as a manager in the lower divisions, but in 1991 Knowles died of a brain tumour aged just 47.

4. Alan Mullery, midfielder

"Come on the Tank," yelled someone from the crowd as Alan Mullery took a throw-in. That was his turning point. "It was not being compared to Danny Blanchflower that bucked me up," says Mullery. "I'm not sure whether he meant it as a compliment or not, but it gave me an identity at last." Comparisons with Blanchflower were pointless of course. By his own admission, Mullery wasn't laden with silky skills, but had "a lot of bustle and energy". Mullery bustled to a consistently excellent level, though, and became an England regular, giving a sterling performance in the 1970 World Cup. He was also named Footballer of the Year three seasons after Spurs sold him back to Fulham in 1972. When Dave Mackay left in 1968, Mullery took over the captaincy: he was a great motivator and strong critic. "With Spurs we could do with a bit more of the killer instinct," he said in 1972. "Players go out when we're playing sides at the bottom of the league in a complacent frame of mind. I think this is diabolical when they're receiving such good wages." What price a modern Mullery?

5. Mike England, centre-back

Mike England had a big, flat shovel forehead for batting balls with. He used it to tidy everything up in central defence and to attack set pieces. When Spurs were chasing a game, he carried his strapping frame into attack, something he relished after a six-game run as a centre-forward when he scored twice alongside Jimmy Greaves in 1968/69. In defence, he could kill a punted ball dead or send dangerous passes through to his front men. Though his tackling could seem a mite clumsy, he was surprisingly fast. Bill Nick preferred him to Ron Henry in his dream Spurs XI and Matt Busby was also in for him when he signed for Spurs in 1966. The 1967 FA Cup final and 1972 UEFA Cup final showcased the best of England but in 1975, at 32, he suddenly retired. Why? Differences with Terry Neill? A lack of appetite for relegation? A feeling his timing had gone? Whether all or none of that is true, England was gone.

6. **Phil Beal**, centre-back

Spurs fans get edgy when they see a ball passed backwards, so Phil Beal's safety-first pushes back to Pat Jennings got the odd back up. But ultimately his game zipped together nicely with centre-back partner Mike England and, over 417 games, Beal could scarcely be faulted. England did the aerial work, while Beal dealt with nippier opponents. Beal's initial chance came after Maurice Norman's horrific leg break in 1965, but Beal in turn broke his arm and was then shifted around the defence on his comeback. Dave Mackay's departure in 1968 provided a barbed opportunity: the chance to establish himself in the biggest pair of empty boots in Tottenham history. But Beal's good control and sharp football brain won the fans round, though they perhaps noticed him most when he'd gone and the dangerous situations he used to quietly defuse reared their heads on the slide into relegation.

7. **Alan Gilzean**, striker

Alan Gilzean used to soak his boots in hot water before games to make them soft so he would have extra sensitivity. The famous headers were just as dextrous: delicate flicks and glancing deflections in whatever direction was required. Though he was a centre-forward when Spurs bought him, his positional sense and awareness made him the perfect support for Jimmy Greaves and then Martin Chivers. Gilly, the King of White Hart Lane, was never fazed. Criticism, fouls or slow-wittedness from his team-mates left him unruffled. None of his team-mates really knew what he did outside of the game, aside from indulging a prodigious lone drinking habit. He could have moved to Sunderland for more money, but chose Spurs because he thought he'd enjoy his football more.

8. **Steve Perryman**, central midfielder

Steve Perryman found himself in an unusual situation at the end of 1971/72. He'd scored two stunning goals in the first leg of the UEFA Cup semi-final against AC Milan and when the team arrived in Italy for the second leg, the 20-year-old found legions of admiring Inter fans waiting for him. But, says Perryman, "It didn't go to my head. I was too much of a defender for that." He was lucky just to

> PERRYMAN CAME INTO THE TEAM AGED 17 AND JUST STAYED THERE WITH SCARCELY A GLITCH FOR 17 YEARS

have had the chance to score at all: Bill Nick had been thinking of dropping him due to poor form. How incongruous to see 'Perryman' and 'poor form' in the same sentence. Perryman came into the team in 1969 aged 17 and just stayed there, with scarcely a glitch, for 17 years. In his early-1970s incarnation, he was a buzzing, harrying, ball-winning midfielder, launching moves with simple passes, his technical skills hidden underneath all the buzzing and harrying.

9. Martin Chivers, centre-forward

Martin Chivers was all yins and yangs: strong and delicate; powerful and skilled; brilliant and anonymous. When he joined from Southampton in January 1968, there were goals galore. Then he faded. Then he was injured (a severed knee ligament) and out of the game for a year. When he came back he was terrible. The following season, 1970/71, he scored 29 goals. But in 1971/72 he was sometimes good, sometimes bad. When he was bad, so were Spurs (perhaps because of the weight of responsibility on Chivers at the head of a 4-3-3 formation). Or was it the other way round? As Ralph Coates says, "whether he didn't get the service or whether he wasn't trying to get the service, only Martin knows." But everyone, even Big Chiv, agreed he lacked fight. Bill Nick goaded him and ordered Mike England and Colin Lee to work him over in training, trying to spark him off. Terry Neill tried the kid-glove approach, which worked, but only temporarily. He could look lazy, because he rationalised chances and didn't run for balls he couldn't get. But at his best he could run like a steam train, shrugging off defenders, then curl a beautiful delicate shot.

10. Martin Peters, midfielder

Martin Peters was appreciated but not quite loved. The qualities of intuition and positional awareness that led Alf Ramsey to say Peters was ten years ahead of his time were difficult to pick up on from the terraces: intuitive drifting into space, a pass, a run. The quality of his technique was clear though: his touch was sweet, his finishing deadly and his aerial game impressive. Some fans would have liked to see more battling, but, said Bill Nick's assistant Eddie Bailey: "Martin is not aggressive in a physical sense, but it's so obvious he wants to win." Peters was tactically astute too, and when Mullery left he took over the captaincy. But like Chivers and England, he didn't see eye to eye with Terry Neill and in 1974 he moved to Norwich where he excelled in the position he had supposedly refused to play in for Neill.

11. Ralph Coates, winger

Ralph Coates is why Matt Le Tissier stayed at Southampton. Coates left a team built around him at Burnley and drowned in the larger pond that was Spurs. The fans were uncharacteristically patient during a poor first season, probably because he always gave his all, and voted him player of the season the next campaign. Mostly, though, Coates's seven seasons were good and only occasionally great. He had decent control and acceleration and a nice line in body swerves, but his shooting was poor and he admits he was over-awed. Coates had been excelling in a free role at Burnley when Bill Nick paid a national record £190,000 for him in 1971 and says he always assumed Nicholson would play him the same way. At Spurs he was played on the wing and found he couldn't get into the game. His best season – 1973/74 – came when he eventually persuaded Nicholson to let him have his head.

THE EXPLOITS OF JAMES PETER GREAVES

"A blinking little genius" – Joe Mercer

1. Off to a flier

Jimmy Greaves messed up on his debut. He'd come too deep to receive Mackay's long throw-in and it arrived at chest height. All he could do was launch himself into a flying scissors-kick and sweet-spot it into the gap he'd already clocked to the left of Blackpool keeper Tony Waiters. In case the White Hart Lane boo boys thought they'd signed a striker with a dodgy sense of positioning he scored another couple of goals later in the game. Spurs won 5-2.

Jimmy Greaves made a scoring debut for every new side he played for:

Southampton Lane Junior School, two goals.

Spurs 1 Chelsea FC 1, one goal. White Hart Lane, 23 August 1957, Division One.

England U23s 6 Bulgaria U23s 2, two goals. Stamford Bridge, 25 September 1957, friendly international.

Peru 4 England 1, one goal. Lima, 17 May 1959, friendly international.

Lanerossi Vicenza 0 AC Milan 3, one goal. Romeo Menti Stadium, 27 August 1961 (Serie A debut).

Spurs 5 Blackpool 2, three goals. White Hart Lane, 16 December 1961, Division One. (Spurs first-team debut).

Manchester City 1 West Ham United 5, two goals. Maine Road, March 1970.

2. Hatfuls

...25 hat-tricks or more in his career, including all four goals in a 4-3 win over Nottingham Forest in his last game for Chelsea. He also scored five for Chelsea against reigning champions Wolves, who were to win the title again that season.

...three four-goal hauls, ten hat-tricks and 48 braces for Spurs.

...six hat-tricks (including two four-goal hauls) for England, one of which came in the 9-3 trouncing of Scotland at Wembley.

3. Golden boots

Jimmy Greaves was Division One top-scorer a record six times, four while at Spurs.

4. Record tallies

In 1960/61 Greavsie scored nearly half of Chelsea's 98 league goals, becoming, at 21, the youngest to bag 100. After arriving at Spurs via Milan, he rattled up 200 league goals by the time he was 23, equalling the record set by Everton's Dixie Dean.

5. Club tallies

Greavsie top-scored for his club in 12 of his 14 seasons in Division One. That includes his first for Spurs, when he arrived in the middle of December 1961. By May he'd scored 21 league goals and 30 in all competitions. As a 15-year-old playing South East Counties League football for Chelsea, he once netted 122 goals in a season.

6. Bevvies
The only thing more prodigious than his goal-scoring was Greavsie's alcohol intake: at his worst, he was putting away 20 pints and two bottles of vodka a day.

7. Ratio awareness
Greaves scored 44 times in 57 England appearances – a goal every 1.3 games. Only Nat Lofthouse can better it. In the league Greaves averaged a goal every 1.45 games.

8. A goalscorer's feast
Greavsie's regular pre-game meal consisted of soup, roast beef, Yorkshire pudding, cauliflower, carrots, peas, three roast potatoes, three large boiled potatoes, steamed pudding and custard. Terry Venables distinctly remembers him scoring five of the goals in a 6-1 victory two hours after one such snack.

9. On the bounce
While Spurs' league form began to buckle under the weight of fixtures as the 1961/62 season wore on, Greavsie kept on scoring. From the 2-2 draw with Bolton on 24 February through to a 4-1 win over Blackburn Rovers on 20 April, he scored in a club-record nine consecutive games (including two braces), though Spurs only managed three wins and four draws from the run.

10. Clairvoyance
"I'd love to win this one tomorrow – that'd give me two Cup final medals," Ron Henry said to Greavsie on the eve of the 1962 Cup final.
"Well, I've got to win tomorrow because I haven't got any," he replied.
"No you ain't, Jim, have you?"
"No, but I'll have one tomorrow because I shall score in a couple of minutes."
Spurs won, set on their way by a Greaves goal after exactly two minutes.

11. For the record
366	league goals (Chelsea 124; Milan 9; Spurs 220; West Ham 13)
35	FA Cup goals (Chelsea 3; Spurs 32)
7	League Cup goals (Chelsea 2; Spurs 5)
3	Inter-Cities Fairs Cup goals (Chelsea)
10	Cup Winners' Cup goals (Spurs)
44	International goals

FAMILY AFFAIRS

The number of brothers, sons, uncles and cousins who've turned out for a schoolboy team here, a reserve team there or the first team once would keep a genealogist quiet for years. Below are those who made any kind of impact on the senior side, plus some illustrious players and their mediocre kinsfolk.

1. Les, Clive and Paul Allen

The Spurs Allens played 492 games for Tottenham, scoring 173 goals. Paul won the FA Cup with Spurs in 1991, having become the youngest-ever winner at 17 with West Ham. Despite his club-record 49 goals in 1986/87, Paul's cousin Clive spent four trophy-less seasons at the Lane. Clive's father Les won two FA Cups, a championship and the Cup Winners' Cup during the 1960s glory years. Paul and Clive's cousin Martin and his father Dennis were also professional footballers.

2. Ray and Stephen Clemence

While Ray was a dab hand between the sticks, opinions were divided on midfield son Stephen. Clem never quite became a first-team regular but he's made a name for himself since joining Birmingham City in 2003.

3. Bobby, Danny and Alex Steel

Bobby was a skilled passer, but also a tricksy dribbler at inside-left for Spurs before World War 1. Younger brother Danny was a gifted centre-half. In January 1910, their little brother Alex made his only appearance at the Lane, playing alongside Bobby and Danny in a 0-0 draw against Bradford City in front of 22,000 fans.

4. John and Andrew Polsten

John and Andrew were the first brothers to play together in a league game for Spurs since the Steels. They formed the centre-back pairing for the last 20 minutes of a 1-0 defeat to Crystal Palace in 1990. John started the game, while Andy replaced John Moncur in the 70th minute. That was Andy's only senior appearance, while John played 28 times and scored once before his move to Norwich.

5. John and Ollie Burton

John and Ollie competed for the centre-half spot for four seasons during Spurs' Southern League years. Ollie eventually ousted brother John, but later turned out to be a much better full-back than centre-half. He played in most of Spurs' games in his new position when they joined the Football League, helping them to promotion.

6. John and Rob McTavish

The brothers played together in Falkirk's forward line for three years, but appeared on the same pitch for Spurs only once. Little else was memorable as Spurs went down 3-0 at Blackburn in front of 14,000 fans in the last game of the 1910/11 season.

7. Glenn and Carl Hoddle

Carl joined Glenn at the Lane between 1983 and 1985. Glenn went on to play for Monaco, won 53 England caps and was ignored for 100 more. Carl didn't trouble the Spurs first team and had spells at Norwich, Bishops Stortford, Leyton Orient (where he made his league debut), Woking, Enfield, Baldock Town and Aylesbury United.

8. David and Gareth Howells

Gareth Howells was nominally a Spurs pro for two years, but was scarcely seen at the Lane between loan spells at Farnborough, Malmo, Enfield, Swindon and Leyton Orient, among others. He left in 1990. While David was pursuing FA Cup glory alongside Gazza, Gareth turned out for Torquay, Dorking, Farnborough, Stockport, Kettering, Hellenic (South Africa) and St Albans City.

9. Alan and Ian Gilzean

Ian Gilzean stuck it out for six years at Spurs without a whiff of first-team action. It's not recorded whether he had a dodgy wispy haircut and a nice line in headers, but he did join his dad's old side Dundee on leaving White Hart Lane in 1992, going onto Doncaster Rovers, Ayr United, Northampton Town and Sligo Rovers.

10. Ron, Steve and Ron Henry

Steve Henry played ten games for the Spurs youth side in 1972/73. His son Ron turned out for Spurs schoolboys in 1999, but didn't managed to win a league title, two FA Cups and a Cup-Winner's Cup like his grandad did in the 1960s.

11. Jimmy and Danny Greaves

When your dad's Jimmy Greaves it's probably best not to try to be a footballer. But Danny did, playing for Spurs juniors and later for Southend and Cambridge United. He did a spot of youth coaching at Southend before managing Halstead Town.

THE FIRST 11 MILLION-POUND MEN

Were they worth it? You do the math…

1. Paul Stewart   £1.7 million
2. Paul Gascoigne   £2 million
3. Gary Lineker   £1.2 million
4. Gordon Durie   £2 million
5. Darren Anderton   £2 million
6. Teddy Sheringham £2.1 million
7. Colin Calderwood £1.25 million
8. Jason Dozzell   £1.9 million
9. Jürgen Klinsmann £2 million
10. Ilie Dumitrescu £2.6 million
11. Gica Popescu   £2.9 million

THE FIRST 11 SEASONS

From humble beginnings

1. 1882/83 Spurs are officially formed on 5 September 1882, the date when the first subscriptions were paid by the founders. Spurs lose 2-0 to the Radicals in their first ever game on 30 September. They later lose 8-1 to Edmonton schools side Latymer.

2. 1883/84 August 1883: local Bible reader John Ripsher holds a meeting to formally establish the club and the 21 boys present vote him in as club president.

3. 1884/85 Hotspur FC officially become Tottenham Hotspur Football Club. A club minute from April 1985 shows the stationmaster at the Park Railway Station (now Northumberland Park) was given a present for looking after the team's goalposts.

4. 1885/86 Spurs enter the London Association Cup and 400 watch them beat St Albans 5-2. They are thrashed 8-0 in the next round by the famous Casuals, but it's a good season overall – Spurs win 24 of their games, scoring 111 goals.

5. 1886/87 Spurs lose 6-0 to Upton Park in the first round of the London Association Cup, but make it to the semi-finals of the East End Cup where they lose to London Caledonians in a replay.

6. 1887/88 Enter only the London Senior Cup and lose 6-0 to Hendon in round one.

7. 1888/89 Spurs move to Northumberland Park, their first ground (they had previously played on Tottenham Marshes), paying an annual rent of £10. It cost 3d (1.25p) to watch a game. Spurs lose in the first round of the London Senior Cup and Middlesex Senior Cup but now play adult rather than boys' football.

8. 1889/90 Spurs go out in the first round of the London Senior Cup yet again but make it to round two of the Middlesex Senior Cup, only to be beaten 4-2 by Clapton.

9. 1890/91 A new high – Spurs reach the second round of the London Senior Cup and Middlesex Senior Cup but are knocked out by Millwall Athletic and Clapton.

10. 1891/92 Spurs make it all the way to round three of the London Senior Cup, losing 4-1 to City Ramblers.

11. 1892/93 Spurs taste league football after joining the Southern Alliance. They finish third, but not all clubs can fulfil their fixtures and the competition peters out.

FOOTBALLERS OF THE YEAR

11 Spurs who won the respect of the press and their peers

1. Danny Blanchflower 1957/58 Football Writers' Player of the Year
Many say this was the finest season in a superlative career, but modest Blanchflower accorded one small paragraph of his autobiography to the 1957/58 campaign: "We had a bad start to the season but then recovered, and after losing in the fourth round of the Cup to Sheffield United, we sprinted home to finish third in the league table behind Wolves and Preston. I had a good year with Tottenham and the Northern Ireland team and I received the Player of the Year award."

2. Danny Blanchflower 1961 Football Writers' Player of the Year
Spurs were thrilling and Blanchflower was captain of the team in name and spirit, pulling the strings, controlling the tempo, dispensing shrewd and lethal passes.

3. Pat Jennings Football Writers' Player of the Year 1973
Jennings reckons he might have been a better keeper if he'd been coached from a young age. That's a scary thought, but then no one would have taught Jennings to keep goal in the unconventional style that proved so effective, and which helped Spurs to two League Cups and a UEFA Cup in the run-up to his first Player of the Year accolade.

4. Pat Jennings Players' Player of the Year 1976
How many players have been voted their country's best while toiling under the threat of relegation?

5. Glenn Hoddle Players' Young Player of the Year 1980
There's something very Spurs about having a bad season (finishing 14th) and still possessing a player voted best in his class. Hoddle scored 22 goals from midfield in 1979/80, including some no human being should be able to score from anywhere.

6. Steve Perryman Football Writers' Player of the Year 1982
Consistent, durable, hardworking: Perryman was everything Spurs have never been. It seems somehow fitting he should have to wait 13 years after his Spurs debut to be voted Player of the Year. By 1982 he had moved from midfield to full-back and found the right-back berth the perfect position for exploiting his tenacity and ball skills.

7. Clive Allen 1987 Players' and Writers' Player of the Year
The man scored 49 goals. Who else would you pick?

8. Gary Lineker Football Writers' Player of the Year 1992
Where would Spurs have been without Gary Lineker in 1991/92? Considering they finished 15th and he scored more than half their league goals, relegated is the most likely answer. With his move to Grampus Eight already announced, he had nothing to prove but proved it anyway. Passengers don't score 35 goals a season.

9. Jürgen Klinsmann Football Writers' Player of the Year 1995
He scored 29 goals, but that's not important. Graceful, stylish, handsome, articulate, predatory but unselfish, charismatic but humble, Klinsmann became a Tottenham legend in ten glorious months. The players voted for the bread-and-butter goals of Alan Shearer, but the writers couldn't help but be seduced by the romance of it all.

10. David Ginola Football Writers' and Players' Player of the Year 1999
Tottenham has a funny effect on managers. Why else would pragmatist Gerry Francis buy a glorious, unpredictable winger and perpetual bore George Graham continue to play him? For all Ginola buried the ball in the upper tiers of the Paxton and Park Lane ends, the fans loved him as a beacon of flair in a Gooner-esque world.

11. Beyond these shores
No Spur has ever claimed the Ballon d'Or or World Player of the Year award, but some have come close. Lineker and Klinsmann finished third in 1991 and 1995 respectively. Jimmy Greaves was third in the Ballon d'Or in 1963.

GLORY GLORY HALLELUJAH: THE DOUBLE TEAM

"It was so simple the way we played. We never got caught in possession. We never tried to beat people. It was look up, pass and move. And you can't stop it." Ron Henry

1. Bill Brown, goalkeeper
Bill Brown sold himself to Bill Nicholson with his performance against England at Wembley in 1959 and a Ted Ditchburn-shaped hole was filled. Well, half-filled: Brown was a waif by comparison, albeit a tall one. His one weakness was crosses, otherwise he was hard to fault. His concentration was intense and he turned in huge performances in Spurs' European games following the Double.

2. Peter Baker, right-back
"Peter may have played football quietly and efficiently but he also played the game as if someone had just hit his mother with a five iron." That's a splash of Greavsie embellishment, but it's true Baker had a warm 'getting to know you' tackle for every winger. "He has to know I'm there," Baker protested. But mostly he liked to shepherd opponents out of harm's way and wait for cover. It might have been a safety-first tactic: Danny Blanchflower's wanderings often left him with both a winger and an inside-forward to look after. Baker was a good foil to the skilful Ron Henry and they were the most consistent performers in the side.

3. Ron Henry, left-back
There was Mackay, there was Blanchflower, there was Cliff Jones. Jimmy Greaves had scored 74 goals in a season and a half. But in the two campaigns after the Double the Spurs Supporters' Club voted Ron Henry player of the season. His quality was between his ears as much as in his feet. The 1961 Cup final was his hour: "I studied [right winger] Howard Riley and it came to me: let him have the ball and he'll make his own mistakes. He'd knock it a little too far in front of him, he'd knock it over the byline. He would go by and come back and get beaten again and I loved it." Henry was very left-footed and his speed of turn had something of the Gary Doherty to it, but his sliding tackles and clever positioning repelled most wingers' tricks.

4. Danny Blanchflower, right-half

"Danny Blanchflower was superb, a sleek Afghan hound among a field of barking terriers, slowing the game down and forcing us to take control." Dave Mackay was remembering the title-clincher against Sheffield Wednesday in April, but it could have been any game, training session, team talk, radio debate or just a day in the life. Blanchflower's football was a projection of his mind: eloquent, confident and apt to tie its opponent in knots. With graceful long and short passes, he kept his fingers on the volume knob of games, always demanding the ball. Bill Nick maintained he was a luxury in a poor side "but in a good side, his creativity, his unorthodox approach was priceless." He was 34 when Spurs did the Double – and though waif-like, he could not be muscled out of games. With Dave Mackay he was the core of the team.

5. Maurice Norman, centre-half

Big Mo Norman would lollop up the centre of the pitch with all the grace of a heavyweight Carlton Palmer. He didn't score hatfuls of goals when he got there, but he sure put off a defender or two. Mostly, he was insurance against Dave Mackay and Danny Blanchflower's wanderlust. There was just too much of Maurice to be whipping the ball off attackers' feet or turning on a sixpence, but surprising speed and anticipation made up for it and his legs were forever snaking out to make unlikely interceptions. Sadly, one of those mighty pins unexpectedly proved to be breakable and Norman's career was ended in a friendly against a Hungarian Select XI in 1965 when it broke in five places.

6. Dave Mackay, left-half

The Spurs training gym had red, yellow, blue and white lines running round the walls. "Chip the ball against the blue line, catch it on your thigh, bounce it on the red line, volley it against the yellow line, bounce it down on your chest, then your head, volley it against the white line and as it comes down, kill it dead." That was the sort of exercise assistant boss Eddie Bailey liked to pull. While the team tried to fathom what he'd said, Mackay had done it: "Do you mean like that, Eddie?" Bill Nick said Mackay was Spurs' greatest ever player. In 1962, Eusébio called him the best all-round player in the world. This has to be said to stave off the myth – grown around the Bremner incident – that he was just a better class of hardman. His tackling was ferocious but fair. He was a surging, ball-winning, attacking force but Bill Nick recalled how he also brought a determined intensity to every part of club life.

7. Cliff Jones, winger

Everyone remembers Cliff Jones sliding along on his chin. Full-backs had to trip him to stop him and he was so fast the momentum carried him for yards. He had the ball control really fast wingers often lack and even at just 5ft 7in he was one of the best headers in the team. He could play on either flank, but liked to cut in from the left on his right foot or leave the touchline and create panic through the middle. His immunity to fear coupled with his speed added up to a long injury list. He played only 29 games in the Double season, with Terry Medwin filling in. Juventus offered £100,000 for him after he dismantled their Serie A-winning defence in a pre-season friendly, but Bill Nick was unmoved. Jones was easily the most thrilling player in his team and possibly the best winger in the world.

8. John White, inside-right

"John White was the Hoddle of his time," says Cliff Jones. "He had all the great skills, the control, the craft; possibly he made himself a little more available than Glenn did. Every time he picked the ball up he always had one pass on." Moves never floundered with White constantly on the move in pursuit of space. He was a facilitator for the team, a role so subtle fans might not notice it, but his team-mates knew it was invaluable. When White was killed by lightning on an Enfield golf course in July 1964, Danny Blanchflower had just retired. White was set to take his place.

9. Bobby Smith, centre-forward

Bobby Smith once frightened off Slovan Bratislava's left-half with nothing more than a raised finger and an icy stare. Bobby was well 'ard, but Bill Nicholson wouldn't have let a player with nothing else to offer sully his Double side. Smith's delicate chip over the Spanish goalkeeper when playing for England in 1960 is an example of his softer side. He could cushion the ball sweetly and lay off weighted passes, and Jimmy Greaves credits him with an important part in his goal haul. Smith scored a goal every game and a half: not a record you can achieve with brute force.

10. Les Allen, inside-left

Les Allen was signed from Chelsea in December 1959. In January he scored two goals in a 3-0 win over Arsenal. In February he scored five in Spurs' record 13-2 win over Crewe in the FA Cup. By May he'd scored 15 goals in 19 games for Spurs. His subtle movement produced regular, unremarkable goals, but he was more than a poacher and worked hard for the team. Allen's goal – the only one of the

> **BOBBY SMITH ONCE SCARED OFF A LEFT-HALF WITH NOTHING MORE THAN A FINGER AND AN ICY STARE**

game against Sheffield Wednesday – was the perfect title-clincher, a spectacular waist-high volley. He lacked a touch of pace, but was strong and comfortable on the ball, a clever player with a stinging shot. Only a footballing genius would deserve to be in the team ahead of him. Jimmy Greaves was that genius.

11. Terry Dyson/Terry Medwin, wingers
If you rolled the talents of Dyson and Medwin into one, you'd have the ideal 11th member of the side. As it was, they were forever competing for the same place. Dyson prevailed in 1960/61 but Medwin played enough games to claim a winner's medal. Dyson was all graft, determination and enthusiasm; Medwin was careful, accurate and thoughtful. Dyson played on the left, Medwin on the right (with Jones switching wings to suit). Fans would have preferred the more cultured Medwin, but the team had culture to burn. Maybe it needed Dyson to buzz and be a nuisance.

GOAL GLUTTONS

Top scorers of hat-tricks and higher

1. Jimmy Greaves 1961-70	13	
2. George Hunt 1930-37	12	
3. Bobby Smith 1955-64	11	
4. Johnny Morrison 1932-39	10	
Cliff Jones 1958-68	10	
6. Ted Harper 1928-32	6	
Martin Chivers 1967-76	6	
8. Frank Osborne 1923-31	5	
Bert Bliss 1911-23	5	
10. Gary Lineker 1989-92	4	
11. Jimmy Cantrell 1912-23	3	
Len Duquemin 1947-58	3	
John Duncan 1974-79	3	
Clive Allen 1984-88	3	
Teddy Sheringham 1992-97, 2001-03	3	

GREAT CAPTAINS

11 inspirational leaders

1. Danny Blanchflower
If the captaincy didn't mean being in charge, it wasn't worth having. Blanchflower demanded the freedom to change tactics as the flow of the game required and had the knack of making both players and management believe he was their man.

2. Gary Mabbutt

What more faithful skipper could there be? He managed to make light of his diabetes and having his cheekbone smashed by Fash. He played all over in the Tottenham cause and kept a steady ship during the chaotic times of Scholar, Venables and Sugar.

3. Ron Burgess

When Arthur Rowe arrived with his new-fangled push-and-run scheme in 1949, Ron Burgess was a Spurs stalwart of ten years' standing and captain of Wales. But he took Rowe's ideas on, and with Alf Ramsey, carried them on to the pitch. When Rowe saw his penchant for carrying the ball upset the balance, Burgess curbed it. He soon skippered Spurs to promotion and the Division One championship.

4. Bobby Buckle

Bobby Buckle was about 14 when he became Spurs' first elected captain in 1882. A committee member from 1884, treasurer from 1890 and member of the first board of directors in 1898 three years after retiring, he helped carry the club from boys' team to FA Cup winners.

5. Steve Perryman

Steve Perryman MBE: 17 years a Spur, ten years a captain. Perryman, who took on the captaincy when Martin Peters left in 1975, played in two great teams a decade apart, and captained Spurs back out of Division Two in between. He won more medals with Spurs than anyone, but nowhere was there a steadier, less inflated ego.

6. Dave Mackay

"Spurs Give Leicester Severe Thrashing – Mackay The Master Is Great Inspiration". So read the headline in the *Daily Telegraph* when Dave Mackay returned to the Spurs team as captain in the first game of the 1965/66 season after two broken legs. Mackay's whirlwind will to win arrived at Spurs in 1958 like a kick up the backside.

7. Alan Mullery

Alan Mullery's drive meant as much to Spurs as his footballing prowess. His criticism prodded team-mates on to greater things and on the pitch he set a Duracell bunny-style example. He took over as skipper when Dave Mackay departed for Derby in 1968 and captained Spurs to a UEFA Cup and two League Cups.

8. John L. Jones

Tactically shrewd, well-built and a formidable link-man at left-half, veteran Jack Jones captained Spurs to the 1901 FA Cup final and continued to inspire the side until he was nearly 40, when, in 1904, he left for Watford.

9. Arthur Grimsdell

The great wing-half never stopped running and never gave up. When he came back from the war, Spurs won Division Two in his first full season, 1919/20, the FA Cup the following year, and then finished as runners-up in Division One. When he broke his leg in October 1925, Spurs were top. Without him they caved in and wound up 15th.

10. Martin Peters

Alan Mullery's hustling, bustling captaincy gave way to Martin Peters' shrewdness. But if Peters's game was more subtle, his will to win was just as fervent.

11. Jamie Redknapp

With Redknapp taking on the 'sicknote' mantle from Darren Anderton, he was more of a professional club captain than a professional footballer, but he was an invaluable one, helping, advising, playing dad and doing his best to gel the team back together as fast as Glenn Hoddle and David Pleat were pulling it apart.

GREAT SCOTS

From north of the border to north London

1. Dave Mackay born: Edinburgh

A football world beyond Heart of Midlothian? Before Bill Nick travelled up to Edinburgh, Dave Mackay had not imagined one. He'd inspired Hearts to success not heard of for 50 years nor ever again. His only brush with the global game had been cruel on an international rookie: against the Spain of Alfredo di Stefano, Ladislao Kubala and Paco Gento, Mackay replaced Scots legend George Young. It finished 4-1 to Spain; Mackay felt "like an old shire horse trotting up alongside Shergar." Mackay scored three of his international goals against Austria and Norway. The fourth launched a stillborn comeback when England crushed Scotland 9-3 at Wembley. Mackay played one last match for Scotland after his fabled leg breaks, in a home international: Jock Stein was the boss, Northern Ireland the opposition. Spurs provided both goalkeepers (Brown and Jennings) and both Scottish goals, scored by Alan Gilzean in a 3-2 Scottish defeat.

2. John White born: Musselburgh, Midlothian

White rose from Musselburgh Juniors through Bonnyrigg Rose Athletic to Falkirk, where Scotland began to take note. Scottish team-mate Dave Mackay was one of those impressed by White's intelligent international debut, when he scored in a 3-2 friendly win over West Germany. Five months later he was a Spurs player.

3. Bill Brown born: Arbroath
A 20-year-old Bill Brown helped Dundee to their first trophy in 41 years when they beat Rangers 3-2 in 1951. He was capped at schoolboy, Under-23 and B-team levels, but had to wait another seven years for his Scotland debut against France in the 1958 World Cup. He was spared Scotland's 9-3 drubbing by England in 1961, when Celtic's Frank Haffey replaced him in goal to disastrous effect, but did play in the thrilling 2-2 draw between England and Scotland at Wembley in 1965.

4. Alan Gilzean born: Coupar Angus, Perthshire
Alan Gilzean scored two goals at White Hart Lane for a Scots XI in a memorial match four months after John White's death. A month later he signed for Spurs, leaving a Dundee side that had won the title and reached the European Cup semi-finals with the aid of his prolific goalscoring. As he crossed the border he metamorphosed from centre-forward to best supporting artist – to Jimmy Greaves, then Martin Chivers. Gilzean made his Scotland debut in a 6-1 friendly win over Norway (Dave Mackay scored two of the goals), but never played for Scotland in a major final.

5. Steve Archibald born: Glasgow
Archibald became the most expensive Scot ever to cross the border in May 1980. The £800,000 bought a track record: a Scottish Second Division championship with Clyde; two League Cups and a Scottish title with Aberdeen. In March, Archibald had scored on his Scottish debut within 20 minutes of replacing Kenny Dalglish in a European Championship qualifier, in a 4-1 rout of Portugal.

6. John Cameron born: Ayr
Spurs' first great manager learnt his classic Scottish dribbling technique and cute passing at Ayr Parkhouse and Queens Park before passing through Everton on his way to Spurs. There, after just nine months, he was promoted to player-manager in 1899. He returned to his home town to coach Ayr United after a spell in Germany as coach of Dresden FC.

7. Peter McWilliam born: Inveravon, Banffshire
Internationals were fewer and further between at the turn of the 20th century so eight caps were something to boast about when Spurs' great manager-to-be was terrorising right-backs. McWilliam was on Albion Rovers and Inverness Thistle's books before signing for Newcastle. He never scored for Scotland and was on the winning side only twice at a time when England and Wales were Scotland's only opposition.

8. John Duncan born: Lochee, Angus
A League Cup with Dundee and an appearance for the Scottish League against the

Football League: John Duncan arrived at Spurs in 1974 without a glittering haul of honours or a dazzling armoury of skills, but produced a steady, unstinting stream of goals in one of Spurs' darkest spells.

9. David Copeland born: Ayr

Scots were ten-a-penny at Spurs at the turn of the century, but the winger-turned-inside-forward from Ayr Parkhouse was special. His inspiring role in Spurs' 1900 Southern League and 1901 FA Cup wins left the Scotland selectors cold, though. In one of Scotland's more fertile attacking eras, Copeland managed only an appearance for the Anglo-Scots against the Home Scots in 1903.

10. Richard Gough born: Stockholm

Spurs lost a player born in Sweden and raised in South Africa because his family were homesick for Scotland. Gough, born of a Scottish mother, already had 26 caps, a Scottish PFA Player of the Year award and a World Cup campaign to his credit when he arrived from Dundee United in 1986. He took his huge talents back north to Ibrox after one season, going on to play over 400 games for Rangers. He was voted Scottish Writers' Player of the Year in 1989, and went on to impress in Scotland's 1990 World Cup campaign.

11. Graeme Souness born: Edinburgh

If Spurs had paid a handsome transfer fee to prise Graeme Souness from a Scottish club, they would surely never have let him go after just 20 minutes of senior football. The Spurs youth player didn't appear on the Scottish club scene until his international career – including three World Cup campaigns from 1978 to 1986 – was over, joining Rangers as player-manager and continuing his magpie-style attitude to silverware.

> GOUGH TOOK HIS HUGE TALENTS BACK NORTH TO IBROX AFTER ONE SEASON, GOING ON TO PLAY 400 GAMES

HARD MEN

Only have a go if you're sure you're hard enough

1. Dave Mackay
2. Bobby Smith
3. Sandy 'Terrible' Tait
4. Graham Roberts
5. Paul Miller
6. Terry Naylor
7. Pat van den Hauwe
8. Neil Ruddock
9. Don McAllister
10. Harry 'Tiger' Erentz
11. Graeme Souness

HAT-TRICK HEROES

11 players who got to keep the ball

1. Cliff Jones When Spurs wiped the floor with Gornik Zabrze at White Hart Lane in the European Cup, Cliff Jones scored a perfect hat-trick – with his right foot, left foot and head. The goals came one after the other (goals two to four) in the 8-1 win, all within 15 minutes. "It was one of the greatest moments of my life," says Jones.

2. Martin Peters In October 1972, 52,000 saw Spurs wallop Manchester United 4-1 at Old Trafford. Martin Peters scored all four.

3. Rocket Ronny Three goals of the season packed into one 40-minute spell after coming off the bench with his team 2-0 down in a seriously uninspiring cup tie against Southampton. Two-two at full time, 6-2 after extra time. Absolute magic.

4. Frank Osborne Bagged three in three successive league games in 1925: against Liverpool at White Hart Lane (Spurs won 3-1); at Leicester Fosse, when Spurs lost 5-3; and against West Ham at the Lane (Spurs won 4-2).

5. Jürgen Klinsmann After a season of treading water just above the relegation zone under Christian Gross in 1997/98, the pressure found relief in spectacular fashion as Wimbledon were trounced 6-2 in the penultimate game of the season, Klinsmann's four-goal haul finally securing safety.

6. Dave Mackay His only hat-trick for Spurs came in a 4-4 draw with Ron Greenwood's bright young Hammers at White Hart Lane in December 1962.

7. Terry Dyson After scoring a brace against West Ham in August 1961, Terry Dyson netted a hat-trick in a 4-3 home win against Arsenal. He's the only Spurs player to put three past the Gooners in a major competition.

8. Alfie Conn Made the long haul up to Newcastle worthwhile for the travelling fans, who saw him dazzle with his skills, and score a hat-trick on his full debut.

9. Nayim The Spurs pendulum has always swung pretty fast, but March 1993 was exceptional. After a 6-0 drubbing by Sheffield United, Spurs went to Maine Road in the FA Cup quarter-final. Nayim completed his hat-trick in the dying minutes, after which the Manchester City fans invaded the pitch, Terry Phelan scored one of the goals of the season (to make it 4-2) and Teddy Sheringham missed a penalty.

10. Bobby Smith When Smith joined Spurs in December 1955 they looked a good bet for the drop. Also struggling were Huddersfield Town and Sheffield United – the opponents in two of Spurs' last three games. The Huddersfield game was lost 2-1; a draw at the next game in Cardiff brought hope, but it was Bobby Smith's hat-trick against the Blades on the last day of the season that made certain.

11. Graham Roberts Spurs fans must have had a collective premonition about this game. Why else would 46,827 of them – the highest home crowd of the season – turn out to for a league game against Southampton, if not to watch their favourite hard man, Graham Roberts, score three goals against his hometown club, the team that had once rejected him?

> 52,000 SAW SPURS WALLOP MAN UNITED 4-1 AT OLD TRAFFORD. MARTIN PETERS SCORED THE LOT

HE'S THE NEW PELÉ/GEORGE BEST/RYAN GIGGS…

11 Spurs with that new-boy pressure

1. **Jimmy Greaves** the new Duncan Edwards
2. **Terry Venables** the new Duncan Edwards
3. **Graham Roberts** "a Duncan Edwards-type player" according to Burkinshaw
4. **Gazza** the new Duncan Edwards
5. **Johnny Metgod** the new Glenn Hoddle
6. **Jason Dozzell** the new Glenn Hoddle
7. **Willem Korsten** better than Harry Kewell (this was a compliment at the time)
8. **Gary Doherty** the Ginger Pelé
9. **Matthew Etherington** the new Ryan Giggs
10. **Jonathan Blondell** the new Pavel Nedved/Zinedine Zidane
11. **Goran Bunjevcevic** the Balkan Beckenbauer

11 HODDLE NIT INFESTATIONS

Head-scratching quotes

1. "Performance-wise it has been good all season," muses Glenn. "I'm scratching my head sometimes to see how we have only picked up one away win. A lot of times we have picked up one point when it should have been three, or no points when it should have been one." It's January 2001 and Glenn is preparing to take his Southampton side to White Hart Lane. Curiously, the Saints haven't been achieving the away results they deserve. As it turns out, Southampton put in a match-winning performance, but only manage a point, George Graham's Spurs side thrilling the White Hart Lane faithful with a trademark 0-0 home draw.

2. "They're a hard side to beat at home," says Hod. "I went there last season and got a 2-2 draw with Southampton when we should have won." It's September, Hod is now at White Hart Lane and contemplating a trip to Sunderland.

3. "We shot ourselves in the foot – it was as simple as that," says Hod. "I'm scratching my head wondering how we lost a game we didn't deserve to lose." November and Spurs give a match-winning display away to title-contenders Leeds, but lose 2-1.

4. "I was scratching my head when the decision for a penalty was made even though the tackle was roughly two yards outside the box," says a perplexed Hoddle. Away to Manchester United, Spurs go a goal down, but are still in contention when

Maurizio Taricco appears to tug on Paul Scholes's shirt as he heads towards the Spurs penalty area. Taricco is sent off and Mike Riley awards a penalty. Spurs lose 4-0.

5. "I can't explain it," says a flummoxed Huddle. "I'm scratching my head wondering how we have lost the game." It's September 2002, and a win at Fulham will see Spurs to the top of the table. Spurs cruise to a 2-0 lead. Then Perry's weak block allows Junichi Inamoto to score. Glenn notices there's an ineffective Slovenian running around the pitch and substitutes Milenko Acimovic for Christian Ziege. But Anthony Gardner gives away a penalty and Sylvain Legwinski grabs a stoppage-time winner.

6. "I'm just left scratching my head." Middlesbrough visit White Hart Lane. Spurs are there too apparently, but Doherty, Richards and Thatcher just can't get to grips with those pesky Boro forwards. It ends 3-0 but it could have been five.

7. "I was very disappointed with the way we performed in the first half," says Hoddle. "We put ourselves on the back foot from the first minute. I'm scratching my head to see where that performance came from." Now April, there's a faint whiff of a UEFA Cup spot in the air – but Spurs must beat Manchester City. Anthony Gardner gives away a corner, which is nodded in by the unmarked David Sommeil after just two minutes. On 21 minutes Gardner is robbed by Robbie Fowler to make it 2-0.

8. "To be honest, I couldn't see where that was coming from," says Hoddle. "I'm scratching my head." August 2003 and Hoddle deploys his £12m strikeforce of Helder Postiga, Bobby Zamora and Fredi Kanoute when Fulham visit the Lane. They fail to register but former non-leaguer Barry Hayles scores a double in Fulham's 3-0 win.

9. "We'd signed Frederic Kanoute and Robbie Keane. In the end, I never ever got the chance to play them together," laments Hoddle. "Looking at how Spurs have done since then, perhaps it was a rash decision for me to go. The Tottenham situation ended with me leaving the club just six matches into the season and that leaves you scratching your head a little bit." It's three weeks later and Hoddle is out of a job.

10. "Team meetings were long drawn-out affairs where the players would just be sitting there scratching their heads and trying to work out what he was on about." (former Spurs midfielder Tim Sherwood).

11. "I can assure you I have never sat down with any consortium," insists Hod. "I don't know where it comes from. My first weekend back in football and there's a story I scratch my head about." A year later and Hoddle has joined Wolves. But the press rumours are that Hoddle intends to buy Spurs and appoint himself as manager.

HOD THE ALL-POWERFUL

Moments of omnipotence

1. Goal v Watford, September 1983 He's on the right of the box, about 15 yards out and at a silly angle. A feint, a dainty back-flick to make space, a half-turn and a gentle chip into the corner. Like watching *Swan Lake*.

2. Goal v Manchester Utd, December 1979 Other-worldly edge-of-the-box volley.

3. Goal v Nottingham Forest, October 1979 Aleksic, to Armstrong, to Jones, to Hoddle and into the net from 18 yards – all without touching the ground.

4. Flick v Norwich City, August 1975 Receiving the ball near his own penalty area, Hoddle marks his debut by flipping the ball over a charging Norwich bustler and wheels away with possession as his challenger flails at fresh air.

5. Pass to Crooks v Wolves, 1981 FA Cup semi-final replay A long raking pass, hit with the outside of the left foot, weighted as though he had a set of scales in his boot. Into Crooks's path. Goal.

6. Pass to Archibald v Feyenoord, UEFA Cup second round, first leg 1983/84 Hod's pass like a hot knife; the Feyenoord defence like butter. Archibald benefits.

7. Pass to Galvin v Feyenoord, UEFA Cup second round, first leg 1983/84 You'd have thought Tony Galvin's head was magnetic the way Hod's 30-yard pass was strangely attracted to it. Two-nil.

8. Pass to Galvin v Feyenoord, UEFA Cup second round, first leg 1983/84 If you ever need a ball delivered onto a moving target the size of an orange from 40 yards, Hod's your man. Galvin benefited; Spurs went 4-0 up.

9. Pass to Crooks v Manchester City, 1981 FA Cup final replay There's a gaggle of City defenders between Hod and Crooks. One false move and Crooks will be offside. Hoddle lifts a rich, ice-cream scoop of a pass over the City boys and Crooks buries it.

10. Clean sheet v Manchester United, 9 January 1980 Hod the emergency keeper replaces the injured Milja Aleksic and keeps a clean sheet in a 1-0 win.

11. Tackling v Manchester City, 1981 FA Cup replay Keith Burkinshaw reckons he was Spurs' best ball-winner that day. Who'd've thought it?

HOMEGROWN XI

Locals lads done good

1. Ted Ditchburn
2. Steve Carr
3. Chris Hughton
4. Steve Perryman
5. Sol Campbell
6. Ledley King
7. Bill Nicholson
8. Eddie Bailey
9. Mark Falco
10. Glenn Hoddle
11. Ron Burgess

HOT SPURS READS

11 literary landmarks

1. The Glory Game, Hunter Davies
The Spurs bible and one of the best football books of all-time. Hunter Davies is the fly-on-the-wall every fan has always wanted to be: in the dressing room, in players' homes and at their parties, scouting with Bill Nick and chatting to the directors, the club doctor, the physio and the fans. The devil is in the everyday detail and the telling character portraits that uncover the men inside the footballers.

2. Winning Their Spurs, Jeremy Novick
Spurs' legends pick their most memorable games, but it's really an excuse to hear some great inside stories: how Keith Burkinshaw let Pat Jennings go to Arsenal, the pro- and anti-Archibald dressing room split, and how Gary Lineker duped Cloughie.

3. Greavsie, Jimmy Greaves
A generous handful of Cockernee one-liners and nostalgia but Greavsie brings the the characters alive with a telling touch of modern perspective. The story of his alcoholic years is frank but not especially extensive. Not surprising really.

4. We are Tottenham, Voices From White Lane, Martin Cloake & Adam Powley
It's often the "that's so true!" element that makes stand-up funny. It's what made *Fever Pitch* entertaining enough for a Spurs fan to enjoy. This series of interviews

with fans during the 2003/04 season, recreates that warm fuzzy empathetic feeling without the Goonerism. Cathartic reading for long-suffering Tottenham-ites.

5. Dream On, Alex Finn
Never again will anyone be given the access to a football club that Hunter Davies enjoyed for *The Glory Game*. But Alex Finn does pretty well during 1990/91, exposing the innards of the club, albeit with a more financial focus.

6. Barcelona To Bedlam, Guy Nathan
The story behind Terry Venables's move from Barcelona to Spurs and the fall-out after Sugar sacked him during the summer of 1993. This is a well-researched book with some jaw-dropping revelations of the behind-the-scenes skullduggery.

7. Behind Closed Doors, Irving Scholar
A surprisingly frank account by Irving Scholar of his time as Spurs chairman.

8. Gazza: My Story
Depressing, pathetic, but painfully honest and comprehensive. Hunter Davies is almost always a good read and never takes on an autobiography if he won't be allowed to give the subject the full treatment.

9. The Double And Before, Danny Blanchflower
This autobiography was penned by Danny himself, so you're not left wondering where your subject ends and your 'ghost' begins. Written in 1961, it lets you inside the mind of one the most charismatic and principled characters the game has known. The only regret is the book was written just after Spurs achieved the Double and doesn't include the European Cup and Cup Winners' Cup successes.

10. Venables, Terry Venables and Neil Hanson
If it's Terry Venables the footballer and coach you're interested in, read up to page 297. For Venables's account of the whole rancid Sugar affair, begin at 298. The first half is an interesting read but there is a sense it's there to justify the second half: Venables's chance to tell it his way. But if everything he says is to be taken at face value, Sugar's attitude and the way he treated the club are breathtaking.

11. David Ginola: Le Magnifique – The Autobiography
This is not a work of pious modesty. But if you can stand the narcissism, you'll be rewarded with unrestrained opinions about some of the game's biggest names. Gerard Houllier, Kenny Dalglish and Alan Shearer have their characters especially roundly assassinated, as does George Graham.

IDLE BOASTS: SERIOUS ANORAK MATERIAL

Spurs were…

1. the first team to do the Double – in 1960/61. (Preston in 1889 just doesn't count). This season spawned several statistics, all records at the time: an eight-point winning margin, 31 league wins and an 11-game unbeaten run.

2. the first British team to win a European trophy – the 1963 Cup Winners' Cup.

3. the first club to float on the stock exchange (in 1983).

4. the only non-league club to win the FA Cup (in 1901).

5. the advocates of numbered shirts. Spurs beat Watford 7-1 in their first game in numbered shirts.

6. the only side to field a player capped for England at all levels. No one can match Terry Venables's achievement since amateur internationals have been abolished.

7. the first-ever winners of the UEFA Cup, beating Wolves 3-2 on aggregate.

8. responsible for the first Premiership substitute, Erik Thorstvedt, who replaced Ian Walker in a 2-0 defeat to Coventry City on 19 August 1992.

9. (and are) the third most successful English club in Europe (behind Liverpool and Manchester United) in terms of number of trophies won.

10. winners of every FA Cup replay they appeared in between 1911 and 1971.

11. responsible for the 10,000th Premiership goal, scored by Les Ferdinand.

11. THE INSPIRATIONAL DOUBLE-WINNERS OF 1961

Bill Brown

Peter Baker   Maurice Norman   Ron Henry

Danny Blanchflower   John White   Dave Mackay

Cliff Jones   Bobby Smith   Les Allen   Terry Dyson

The glory glory side, "Super Spurs", call them what you will, this is the definitive line-up from an era when winning the Double wasn't something that happened every other season. You'll find a more detailed memorial to the side on p58.

THE KING OF WHITE HART LANE, ALAN GILZEAN

11 facts about...

1. The best header of a football ever

Gilly was a glancer not a power header – so subtle sometimes you didn't even realise he'd made contact. Against Manchester Utd, in a 2-2 draw in 1970, Cyril Knowles scored with a cross that went straight in. At least, that's what everyone thought until TV highlights showed Gilzean had made a crucial deflection.

2. The near-post glance
A trademark Tottenham move. Corners would be floated in and Gilly would flick them backwards from the near post for Martin Chivers to score.

3. Bald and old...
Always looking ancient, Gilly notoriously didn't have a birth certificate. He was always 30-something even when he was probably still 20-something.

4. ...and slow
But Gilly seemed to have a map of the game in his head and was able to bring players into the game with exquisite touches with both head and feet.

5. A wife, two kids and a budgie

6. The battle of Bucharest
In the UEFA Cup tie against Rapid Bucharest in 1971 the old fella's legendary cool head under intense provocation was tested to infinity and beyond. Punched in the kidneys, legs stamped on, elbowed in the ribs and continually brutalised. The great man's reaction? He shook his head and shrugged.

11. KEITH BURKINSHAW'S 1984 UEFA CUP WINNERS

Tony Parkes

Gary Mabbutt   Paul Miller

Danny Thomas   Chris Hughton

Graham Roberts

Gary Stevens   Micky Hazard   Tony Galvin

Mark Falco   Steve Archibald

The team that beat Anderlecht in the 1984 UEFA Cup final. Spurs throw on Ally Dick, for Mabbutt and Ossie Ardiles for Miller in a desperate – and successful – attempt to save the game

7. Taking defeat to Chelsea in the right spirit
After losing a League Cup semi-final to a freak Alan Hudson last-minute goal he said: "What a f**king goal… I'm definitely not going upstairs. They can stick their reception."

8. Partick Thistle syndrome
Flicking on drop kicks from Jennings, Gilly would head wide to the wings expecting someone to get on the end. "For heaven's sake," Bill Nicholson would say, "hold the ball up for us or else play to feet. You're not playing against Partick Thistle."

9. The long throw
Another trademark Tottenham move. Chivers would hurl the ball huge distances on to Gilly who would flick them backwards, usually for Martin Peters to score.

10. Negotiating skills
Gilly initially turned down Spurs for Sunderland because they offered him £20 for a win and £10 for a draw compared with Billy Nick's offer of £4 and £2. Nicholson told him Sunderland's offer was illegal so Gilly came to Spurs. Nicholson later discovered that Sunderland had been within their rights under new regulations.

11. Healthy attitude to coaching
"Without skill you haven't a chance… I don't rate coaching very high. Any grade of manager or coach will give you that… I look upon training as getting fit to use the skills I've got naturally."

LEAST SUCCESSFUL MANAGERS (BY PERCENTAGE OF WINS)

11 managers who didn't play the percentages

1. Ossie Ardiles	played 65	30.8%
2. Christian Gross	played 29	34.5%
3. Terry Neill	played 89	34.8%
4. Gerry Francis	played 146	38.4%

5. Jacques Santini	played 13	38.5%
6. George Graham	played 125	39.2%
7. Glenn Hoddle	played 104	39.4%
8. Billy Minter	played 124	39.5%
9. Terry Venables	played 165	40.6%
10. Keith Burkinshaw	played 431	42.2%
11. The Directors	played 231	42.6%

LOCAL HEROES

Only eight Tottenham lads have ever played professionally for Spurs. And a motley crew they are. Turns out Edmonton is more of a footballing hotbed with 19 Spurs hailing from up by the North Circular. Included below are three of the best.

1. Arthur Rowe born: Tottenham
Spurs's second-greatest manager was born within a goal kick of the Lane. Mr Push-and-Run signed on as a schoolboy, straying no further than Cheshunt and the Northfleet nursery on his way to the first team. Tried his hand coaching in Hungary but war intervened. Ended up at Chelmsford City before taking charge at Spurs.

2. Jimmy Pearce born: Tottenham
The only other truly local lad of note, Pearce played for Tottenham and England schools before making his debut against Arsenal in 1968. Just as he seemed primed to switch from super-sub to first-team cert, the utility forward was struck down by a rare bone condition. At 26, he was never to play professional football again.

3. Walter Bellamy born: Tottenham
The Leysian Mission, Tufnell Park and Dulwich Hamlet amateur turned pro with Spurs in 1926, making 73 appearances on the wing and scoring nine league goals in as many years before heading off to Brighton.

4. Bill Lane born: Tottenham
Despite the great Spurs name, the nippy centre-forward was no homeboy, playing for 16 different clubs (Gnome Athletic being the most amusing). His 29 Spurs appearances came between 1924 and 1927.

5. Sid White born: Tottenham
Signed from Edmonton Ramblers, the half-back played 22 times for Spurs from 1921 until he retired in 1928.

6. Bert Ringrose born: Tottenham
Went from Northfleet to Notts County via ten Tottenham appearances (1936-7).

7. Walter Moles born: Tottenham
Made three appearances for Spurs from 1900 to 1902 before heading to Waverly.

8. Harry Gilberg born: Tottenham
This 1964 Northfleet graduate played twice before heading west to QPR.

9. Jimmy Dimmock born: Edmonton
Best of the Edmonton posse was 1920s stalwart Dimmock, who scored the 1921 FA Cup-winning goal against Wolves. The former Edmonton Ramblers man had all the superfluous trickery of a good Spurs winger. He made 438 appearances.

10. Tony Marchi born: Edmonton
Local lad but there was plenty that was cosmopolitan about Anthony Vittorio Marchi. He was tempted away from Spurs by the money on offer in his father's homeland, playing for Lanerossi, Torino and Juventus before returning to Spurs, only to find Bill Nick had bought Dave Mackay to play in his position.

11. Les Medley born: Edmonton
After a first spell at Spurs, Medley spent the next few years living closer to the other Edmonton – in Canada, where he played for the Toronto Greenbacks and Ulster United. Returned to be top scorer as Spurs won promotion in 1949/50 and inspired during the ensuing title-winning season.

MAGNIFICENT MIDDLE NAMES

What were their parents thinking?

1. Clive Euclid Aklana Wilson
2. Jason Alvin Winans Dozzell
3. David Desire Marc Ginola
4. Johannes Antonius Bernardus Metgod
5. Martin Harcourt Chivers
6. Terence Kent Dyson
7. Ossie Cesar Ardiles
8. Martin Stanford Peters
9. Dean Ivor Richards
10. Christopher Roland Waddle
11. John Thomas Gavin

"MAKE IT SIMPLE, MAKE IT QUICK": THE PUSH-AND-RUN TEAM

If you try to dribble past three men, you might lose the ball. If you punt it upfield your opponent might win it. But it wasn't until Spurs rocketed from the Second Division to win the title and England were cut apart by Hungary that anyone thought of doing it differently. If your passes are short and accurate, you won't lose the ball. If you want to receive the ball safely you must run into space. It's what underpinned the Spurs team that flummoxed every other side for two seasons. But it needed technique, mobility and brains.

1. Ted Ditchburn, goalkeeper
Ditchburn was the first line of attack, launching passing moves via his full-backs. He never punched or parried where he could catch, was expert at diving at feet, collected crosses with ease, concentrated ferociously and was supremely agile. His reflex saves were honed by a training exercise of continuous throwing and diving at point-blank range. Even Pat Jennings had to suffer comparisons with him.

2. Alf Ramsey, right-back

The rest of the push-and-run team was free, or nearly, but Ramsey cost Spurs a hefty £21,000 from Southampton. In an era when attackers played and defenders tackled, this tells you everything about push-and-run. A cultured ball-player at the back of the team was essential. It also tells you about the great influence of Alf Ramsey.

3. Arthur Willis/Charlie Withers, full-backs

In a team built on links of familiarity, Willis was a bolt-on. He'd featured in just two games in the Division Two promotion season but he played Withers out of the side. As Spurs won the title with fluid, attacking football, Willis helped keep the third-tightest ship in Division One. Withers, solidly built and determined, was one of the Edmonton lads. When Spurs won promotion, less than a goal per game got past his tackles. His reward? Just four appearances as Spurs won the championship.

4. Bill Nicholson, right-half

Bill Nick the manager was a paradoxical beast: a grim Yorkshire tough nut who demanded beautiful football. Bill Nick the player carried a touch of contradiction, too. He did the terrier run – covered, tackled, worked – but had a touch of class. He played only once for England scoring from long range after 30 seconds. How Spurs.

5. Harry Clarke, centre-half (midfield)

Two of the push-and-run side cost a fee. Of those, Harry Clarke's was described as "peanuts". For this paltry sum Spurs got a towering 6ft 3in centre-half, naturally commanding in the air, but equally happy on the ball and adept at distributing it. Clarke was ever-present during push-and-run's two most successful seasons.

6. Ronnie Burgess, left-half

In a team of equals, Ron Burgess and Alf Ramsey were more equal than others. Burgess had a personal cliché: "the team dynamo". Plucked from kickabouts on the slag heaps by the River Ebbw, tested at Spurs and so very nearly sent back to Wales, perhaps he was driven by the thought of "what if…" An instinct for going forward, but a brain for defending. Captain for eight seasons, he made 505 appearances.

7. Sonny Walters, right-winger

Born in Edmonton, signed to Tottenham Juniors, matured in the Finchley nursery side and blossoming for Spurs… but when it came to England, Sonny Walters hit a very thick glass ceiling: Stanley Matthews and Tom Finney. Walters's wing-play was opportunistic, fast and direct and it got him goals: 15 in the championship season when he top-scored and 14 when Spurs won promotion.

8. Les Bennett, inside right

Les Bennett made up for losing his best years to the war in some style. A Londoner, he was tall, upright, elegant and long-striding. But a clever turn and deceptive dribbling technique made him hard to stick to. Created as many goals as he scored.

9. Len Duquemin, centre-forward

The Duke liked to drag his marker out of position to leave space for team-mates, so his seasonal goal tallies seemed unimpressive, though in 11 years he became one of only eight players to score 100 league goals for Spurs. He wasn't extravagantly skilled but had what the team needed: mobility, work rate, timing and positioning. Scored the only goal of the game against Sheffield Wednesday to seal the title.

10. Eddie Bailey, inside-left

With an impeccable first touch and rapid football brain, Bailey was born to push and run. The game plan required him to be a top-notch creator, but he also scored five goals in the first five of his nine games for England.

11. Les Medley, outside-left

Les Medley could be an orthodox winger but preferred to go wandering. And when he did, his unexpected appearance in other parts of the pitch brought goals. The Edmonton lad top-scored in 1949/50 and reached double-figures the following season. He had pace and power, but where Walters was direct, Medley was tricky and unfazed by one-on-ones. With Ron Burgess behind, Medley never wanted for the ball and the partnership the pair formed with Bailey on the left was deadly.

MONEY DOWN THE DRAIN

Almost £50 million flushed away

1. Sergei Rebrov, £11 million

There was definitely a quality player in there somewhere, and Spurs fans never gave up hope, chanting his name when Hod refused to play him during the great striker shortage. It didn't help that we seemed to have bought him as a centre-forward when he'd made his name at Dynamo Kiev as Andriy Shevchenko's support act.

2. Dean Richards, £8.1 million

There was a spell during Dean Richards' Spurs career where, in between the initial season of howlers, the injury and general patches of mediocrity, he actually looked quite good. But he never ever looked £8.1m-worth of good.

3. Helder Postiga, £6.25 million
The press tired of Postie long before the fans lost patience. He had a great anti-Arsenal chant after all. Yet again it seemed Spurs hadn't done their homework, José Mourinho saying Postiga's game didn't suit Spurs' style of play.

4. Ben Thatcher, £5 million
Wimbledon left-back for sale. Uncapped (for Wales), helped take Wimbledon down to the First Division, quite good when he was younger. Offers in the region of £5 million. You wouldn't touch it, would you? Unless you were a Gooner bore-merchant. Thanks George.

5. Tim Sherwood, £4 million
No player should be consigned to the stiffs without hope of first-team football but we weren't pining for him and he was soon re-christened Deadwood. There's a story that Hoddle went to see Daniel Levy and described the ball-winning midfielder the team lacked. Levy reportedly replied that the player sounded like Sherwood.

6. Chris Perry, £4 million
A good squad player, but a mite expensive for a bench-warmer. Was reasonably sound in the centre of defence but had issues over passing the ball to a team-mate.

7. Jason Dozzell, £1.9 million
"How much is that Dozy in the window? I do hope that Dozy's for sale…"

8. Bobby Zamora, £1.5 million
Technically not a complete waste of money as we used him to pay for Jermain Defoe, but he did work out at £250,000 per game.

9. Gary Doherty, £1 million
One million pounds for a man with a turn slower than a tanker, no conception of the offside rule and an unerring knack of committing fatal howlers in his own box.

10. John Scales, £2.5 million
Scalesy wasn't a bad player, but £2.5m for 29 games was hardly value for money.

11. Willem Korsten, £1.5 million
Was supposed to be the business, as his 30-yard screamer against Manchester United suggested, but still cost us £125,000 a game before his career-ending injury.

MOST CAPPED WHILE AT SPURS

11 long-serving internationals

1. Pat Jennings	Northern Ireland	75
2. Chris Hughton	Ireland	51
3. Erik Thorstvedt	Norway	46
4. Glenn Hoddle	England	44
5. Danny Blanchflower	Northern Ireland	43
6. Jimmy Greaves	England	42
7. Cliff Jones	Wales	41
8. Teddy Sheringham	England	41
9. Sol Campbell	England	40
10. Gary Lineker	England	38
11. Chris Waddle	England	36

MOST GOALS CONCEDED IN A SEASON

Like a bucket with a hole

Total	Season	Goals per game	Bottom team's goals against	League position
1. 95	1958/59	2.26	112	18th
2. 93	1934/35	2.21	93	bottom
3. 90	1914/15	2.14	90	bottom
4. 86	1927/28	2.05	88	21st
5. 81	1928/29	1.93	72	10th
6. 81	1945/46	1.93	120	9th
7. 81	1963/64	1.93	121	4th
8. 79	1925/26	1.88	74	15th
9. 78	1926/27	1.86	86	13th
10. 78	1931/32	1.86	78	8th
11. 77	1957/58	1.83	77	3rd

League goals only

MOST GOALS SCORED IN A SEASON

11 seasons to be cheerful

Total	Season	Goals per game	Champions goal haul	League position
1. 115	1960/61	2.74	115	Champions
2. 111	1962/63	2.64	84	2nd
3. 104	1956/57	2.48	103	2nd
4. 102	1919/20	2.43	102	Division 2 champions
5. 97	1963/64	2.31	92	4th
6. 96	1932/33	2.29	78	2nd
7. 93	1957/58	2.21	103	3rd
8. 91	1935/36	2.17	85	5th
9. 88	1930/31	2.1	121	3rd
10. 88	1961/62	2.1	93	3rd
11. 88	1936/37	2.1	89	10th

League goals only

MOST LEAGUE WINS IN A SEASON

It's a win–win situation

1. 32	1919/20	Division 2 Champions
2. 31	1960/61	Champions
3. 27	1949/50	Division 2 Champions
4. 25	1950/51	Champions
5. 24	1959/60	3rd
6. 24	1966/67	3rd
7. 23	1962/63	Runners up
8. 23	1984/85	3rd
9. 22	1951/52	Runners up
10. 22	1956/57	Runners up
11. 22	1930/31	3rd

MOST SUCCESSFUL MANAGERS BY PERCENTAGE OF WINS

Take a bow, gentlemen

1. Frank Brettell	played 63	58.7%
2. Arthur Turner	played 49	55.1%
3. David Pleat*	played 71	54.9%
4. John Cameron	played 570	51.9%
5. Bill Nicholson	played 832	49%
6. Arthur Rowe	played 283	47.7%
7. Fred Kirkham	played 61	47.5%
8. Jimmy Anderson	played 153	47.1%
9. Doug Livermore &		
Ray Clemence	played 51	45.1%
10. Peter Shreeve**	played 177	44.6%
11. Jack Tresadern	played 146	44.5%

*does not include caretaker stints **Combined spells in charge

NICKNAMES

Glenda! Man on!

1. Magic John Pratt. As in "Do some magic – disappear!"
2. Mary Peters Martin Peters. For his aversion to mixing it.
3. Glenda Glenn Hoddle. For his aversion to mixing it.
4. Elastic Milija Aleksic. Why let the quality get in the way of a good nickname?
5. Booby Bobby Mimms. For the quality of his goalkeeping.
6. Dark Horse of the Pampas Ricky Villa.
7. Jukebox Gordon Durie. Also, Groin Strain.
8. Kataklinsmann Jürgen's nickname in Italy for the devastation he caused.
9. Easyjet Steffen Freund. A sponsor in the upper tiers often targeted by his shots.
10. Mushy Matthew Etherington. For a mushroom haircut he had in his teens.
11. Digger Simon Davies. His favourite childhood toy was a little red spade.

NORWICH CITY

Spurs' reject bin number one

1. Martin Peters	Spurs: 1970-75	Norwich: 1975-80
2. Martin Chivers	Spurs: 1967-76	Norwich: 1978-79
(via Servette in Switzerland)		
3. Jimmy Neighbour	Spurs: 1970-77	Norwich: 1977-79
4. Ian Culverhouse	Spurs: 1983-84	Norwich: 1985-94
5. Garry Brooke	Spurs: 1980-85	Norwich: 1985-87
6. Ian Crook	Spurs: 1982-86	Norwich: 1986-97
7. Mark Bowen	Spurs: 1983-87	Norwich: 1987-96
8. John Polston	Spurs: 1986-90	Norwich: 1990-98
9. Paul McVeigh	Spurs: 1996-2000	Norwich: 2000-present
10. Kevin Scott	Spurs: 1993-96	Norwich: 1996-99
11. Gary Doherty	Spurs: 1999-2004	Norwich: 2004-present

NOTABLE PROGRAMMES

Pre-match reading classics

1. 1901 FA Cup final original fixture (the game went to a replay)
The programme for Spurs' first FA Cup win consisted of a single sheet displaying the venue, participating teams, date and kick-off time, officials and team line-ups. The line-ups were arranged in formation: 2-3-5 (there were no variations back then).

2. Spurs v Newcastle United, 7 January 1928, Division One
There was nothing special about this fixture but the programme was a gem. In the days when the club retained an ability to laugh at itself, the programmes always featured cartoons on the front. This one, priced at 1p, showed 'Cocky', a creation of Fred Perry – essentially an early Chirpy – standing with an empty bucket next to a frozen tap. The water tank above the tap was labelled 'Football League Xmas Points' and the sink beneath it 'Spurland'. "Not a drop this Christmas," moans Cocky. Spurs' fortunes never improved: they were relegated that season after finishing 21st.

3. Spurs v Chelsea, 1 February 1930, Division Two
Jos Walker had by now taken over the cartoons from Fred Perry. This one showed Spurs boss Percy Smith and a Chelsea pensioner standing in the countryside looking towards a distant, radiant city with the legend 'First Division' above it. The caption read "The Chelsea Pensioner: 'It's taking a long while to get to reach yonder

City. Would you be kind and give me a helping hand, sir?'" In the event though, Chelsea were promoted and Spurs had to wait another three years.

4. The 1950 Tottenham Hotspur Christmas Programme
Contained a cartoon depicting manager Arthur Rowe sitting with his feet up on the mantelpiece and dreaming of the Double. "He also serves who only sits and waits," read the caption. In the bubble of Rowe's dream, the Spurs team high-step across the pitch, captain Ron Burgess to the fore, beside the caption "… while the Spurs go marching on."

5. Spurs v Liverpool, 5 May 1951
By the 1950s, Spurs' programmes no longer carried cartoons, but this one, for the last game of the club's first Championship-winning season, was an exception. Now costing 2p, it showed an implausibly puffy-chested Spurs team, with Arthur Rowe and Ron Burgess in the centre, shaking hands in front of the Championship trophy. Behind, the cockerel announces it has "something to crow about", while the main caption reads "Our boys do it again."

6. Spurs v Leicester, 6 May 1961, FA Cup final
The occasion was memorable, the programme less so. The cover featured an admittedly very dramatic aerial shot of the stadium with a match in progress.

7. Spurs v Atletico Madrid, 1963 Cup Winners' Cup final
Carried a cartoon of an English footballer (you can tell he's English by the bowler hat and the umbrella hooked over his arm), pretending to be a bull charging towards a Spanish player in matador's hat who holds out the Cup Winners' Cup like a red cape: the holders issuing a 'come and get it' call to the challengers.

8. Wolves v Spurs, 3 September 1969, League Cup second round
For sheer cheesiness, this can't be beaten. The cover, headlined 'Molinews', bore a picture of Cyril Knowles and his brother Peter, a Wolves player who later gave up to be a Jehovah's Witness. Peter shakes hands with Cyril underneath the headline 'Oh Brother… it's the League Cup!' (The triumphant brother was Peter: Wolves won 1-0.)

9. Spurs v Sheffield Wednesday, 3 September 1910
The first programme of the season, dated 1 September 1910 (when Spurs were away to Everton) shows Cocky, hands in pockets large enough for a pocket snooker tournament, talking to a cricketer, heading back to the pavilion. The cricketer says: "Well Cocky, au revoir and I sincerely hope the weather will be kinder to you than it has been with me," to which Cocky replies succinctly: "Carried unanimously".

10. Spurs v Wolves, 6 February 1982
This was the first game after the opening of the new West Stand. The programme, costing 50p, simply carried an imposing picture of the characterless empty stand.

11. Spurs v Leicester City, 21 March 1999, Worthington Cup final
A £5 memento of Spurs most recent – and valueless – piece of silverware bought you such gems as an interview with Leicester keeper Kasey Keller, a 'Pure Gineus' article on our favourite Frenchman, an interview with Lane laundry ladies Margaret and Silvia, and feature pen portraits with Ramon Vega, Andy Sinton and Chris Armstrong.

NOT WORTH THE AIRFARE

Should have bought a return

1. Paolo Tramezzani
Who knows what Christian Gross saw in the 29-year-old left-back, who made just seven appearances in 18 months. Fell out with new boss George Graham when he wanted to return to Italy for surgery on his Achilles tendon. Spurs paid up the final year of his contract and he disappeared into the Italian lower leagues.

2. Kazuyuki Toda
Defensive midfielder Kazu arrived on a year-long loan, played twice, did nothing wrong nor anything especially right, then returned to Shimizu S Pulse.

3. Moussa Saib
A £2.3m signing from Valencia, Saib looked classy in Spurs' skill-starved midfield on his full debut – a 3-1 win against Crystal Palace in March 1998. But he needed a back operation and while he was out George Graham came in. It was a pleasant surprise when Graham retained David Ginola; he was never going to keep Saib too. He was loaned out to Saudi side Al Nasr, before Spurs sold him back to his old club Auxerre.

4. Milenko Acimovic
Milo has taken to French football at Lille, much as the man who brought him to Spurs, Glenn Hoddle, flourished on moving to France. But if Milo was a little in the Hoddle mould, he was not in his league and seemed far too lightweight for the Premiership. After two years on Spurs' books, his loan to Lille was made permanent.

5. Mbulelo Mabizela
Spurs went away on a tour of South Africa in 2003 and came back with the national

captain. But as is often the case with holiday souvenirs, Spurs couldn't figure out where to put him. Helped us scandalously rob Leicester of three points with that piledriver in October 2003 before being released. He then moved to Valerenga in Norway where his new boss said he was too fat.

6. Jonathan Blondel
The 18-year-old Belgian midfielder arrived in July 2002 hailed as a seriously hot prospect. But he was terribly young and terribly homesick and terribly tiny. He asked to go on loan back to Belgium, but Spurs wanted to loan him to an English club to help him adapt to the game. He played in the League Cup thrashing of Coventry and greatly impressed. But eventually the affair was given up as a bad job and Blondel was sold to Bruges.

7. Stéphane Dalmat – except for three games
Glenn Hoddle's departure was bad news for Inter loanee Stéphane Dalmat. David Pleat was unsure what to do with him. Sometimes he started, sometimes he didn't. He had training ground bust-ups with his team-mates. All their fault apparently. Spurs sent him back and promptly loaned him out to Toulouse.

8. Willem Korsten
At the end of 2000/2001, Willem Korsten scored two goals against Manchester United. One was a delicate volleyed lob, the other a strong, low drive. Then doctors told him that if he carried on playing he would end up unable to walk. So ended two seasons of injuries punctuated by hat-tricks and spectacular strikes in the reserves.

9. Goran Bunjevcevic
Bunjevcevic should be at a good continental home where someone will take care of him. A place where he'll have time to use his ball skills, won't be required to tackle too often and can preferably be played in the sweeper role where he made his career at Red Star Belgrade. He's patently not a midfield ball-winner or a centre-back, and, well, we don't play with a sweeper at Spurs.

10. Johnny Metgod
The ex-Real Madrid midfielder had gained a reputation for cultured passing and venomous free kicks while playing for Forest. But Metgod began the season on the bench and managed only three starts before Venables took over. Venables was no more keen than Pleat had been on his own £250,000 purchase and then Metgod got injured and couldn't play anyway. Four end-of-season games completed his Spurs career and he moved to Feyenoord, helping them put Spurs out of the Cup Winners' Cup in 1991/92.

11. Ilie Dumitrescu & Gica Popescu 1994/95

"All Dumitrescu wanted to do was cut in from the left wing and bend the ball into the top right corner," says Teddy Sheringham. "Ilie's attitude was: 'If it works, great. If it doesn't, so what?'" The fans were dazzled when Dumi's skills produced the goods, but when Gerry Francis came in to plumb the goal leak, lazy Romanian showboaters were never going to be first on his list. Popescu wasn't flash; just a very fine reader of the game. Which was of little use as the ball sailed continually over his head during the Francis regime. Proved his worth by going to Barcelona at the end of the season.

THE ONES THAT GOT AWAY

No good crying about it now but...

1. Graeme Souness

For Spurs: 26 minutes at the end of a 9-1 UEFA Cup trouncing of Keflavik.
For Liverpool: five league titles, four League Cups, three European Cups, and an FA Cup. D'oh!

2. David Beckham

According to Venables, he was aware of Spurs schoolboy Beckham but Spurs scout John Moncur told him: "We've been after him but he's Man United-mad." Beckham says: "I think I met Terry Venables once in the two years I was at Tottenham. That doesn't exactly inspire you to join."

3. Kevin Keegan

Spurs scout Charlie Faulkner had received a good report and decided to go and see Keegan for himself. But he'd already arranged a scouting mission to Scotland and missed the last game of the season. In the summer Keegan signed for Liverpool.

4. Richard Gough

At least this one wasn't due to carelessness. Gough was the best since Mike England, working a treat alongside Mabbsey. But the Gough family were pining for Scotland.

5. Des Walker
A junior on Spurs' books, but partly made up for his loss by scoring Spurs' winning goal in the 1991 FA Cup final.

6. Jimmy Seed
The great inside-forward inspired Spurs to their 1921 FA Cup win and promotion in 1920. But after Billy Minter let him go to Sheffield Wednesday, he was instrumental in keeping them in Division One at Spurs' expense.

7. Mario Kempes
Scored a hat-trick against Jordel Blink while on trial during a pre-season tour of Norway and Sweden. Unimpressed (Spurs did score nine), the club rejected him.

8. Peter Taylor
Spurs could have saved themselves a whopping £400,000 in 1976 if they hadn't rejected Taylor as a youngster. They would then have avoided making a £250,000 loss when they sold him to Leyton Orient after he never really made it.

9. Les Allen
Spurs did pretty well out of Double-winner Les Allen in the end, but they could have saved themselves £20,000 if they'd not let him go as a teenage amateur.

10. Jamie Redknapp
If Spurs hadn't released him when he was a schoolboy they might have had his best years instead of his injured ones.

11. Peter Crouch
It remains to be seen if Crouch will be more Shearer or Beattie, but in 2004/05 the former Spurs trainee (1998-2000) was banging in goals like clockwork for Saints.

OWN GOALS

By us, by them, by people in charge

1. Tottenham Hotspur PLC
Irving Scholar and Paul Bobroff turned newly floated Spurs into a 'leisure group.' A company specialising in stadium ticketing systems was bought and, more oddly, two women's clothing companies acquired. The club shop began to sell new ranges of tat and Saatchis was called in to advertise the brave new dream. The profits would

subsidise the football club and the purchase of exciting new players. Only it was the football profits that had to bail out the investments and the exciting new player, one Paul Gascoigne, who had to be sold to stop the whole leaky outfit sinking from view.

2. Gary Mabbutt v Coventry, 1987 FA Cup final

"I go to try to shut Lloyd McGrath down and as he crosses the ball, I put my leg out to stop the cross. It hit me on top of the knee and I watched it loop right over Ray Clemence and into the far corner." No one blames Mabbsey: he'd already scrambled one in at the other end and made up for it all four years later. But the sight of him doubled up in despair after scoring Coventry's winner will always be the memory that endures from the only FA Cup final Spurs ever lost. "Do you realise that's the first time I've chipped a ball all season?" Mabbsey told Ray Clemence as they walked off.

3. Des Walker, Nottingham Forest, 1991 FA Cup final

Funnily enough, it was Mabbsey who Paul Stewart was aiming for when he flicked on Nayim's corner, but Des Walker scored for him, heading Spurs' extra-time winner into his own net. You might think justice had been done, after Lee Glover pushed Mabbutt out of the Forest wall to make way for Stuart Pearce's free kick. But then, if you were a Forest fan you might think Spurs should have been down to ten men.

4. Steve Perryman v Real Madrid, 1985 UEFA Cup fourth round

Why Spurs' longest-serving, most faithful servant should be the one to end the 42-game unbeaten European home record by putting through his own net for the only goal of the tie is something only football's spiteful gods can explain.

5. Dispensing with genius

Glenn Hoddle might have held onto his job a little longer if his side hadn't sorely lacked a midfield ball-winner in the latter stages of his tenure. He had two at the club of course, but Tim Sherwood and Steffen Freund had dared to hint to the press that the Spurs camp wasn't full of happy shiny people. Not one to bury a grudge, Hod dropped them and he and Spurs suffered the consequences.

6. Mike England and John Pratt v Burnley, 5 October 1974

Centre-back Mike England and defensive midfielder John Pratt scored four of the five goals in this game: one each for Burnley in the first half, and one each for Spurs in the second. Unfortunately Burnley scored the decisive fifth goal for themselves.

7. Tommy Clay v Aston Villa, 1919/20 FA Cup fourth round

Own goals seem to happen to all the least deserving players. Clay was Spurs' captain and a brilliant full-back. This was Spurs' first season in Division Two after Arsenal had contrived to have them relegated, so when First Division Aston Villa came to visit there was something to prove. Spurs were proving it very nicely by outplaying Villa until Clay sliced an easy clearance into his own net. Villa went on to win the Cup.

8. Stephen Carr v Kaiserslautern, 1999/00 UEFA Cup second round, second leg
To add the final inglorious touch after George Graham's Spurs had attempted to defend their way to victory, Steve Carr scored the second of Kaiserslautern's two winning goals in the dying minutes.

9. False economy
In November 1926, Spurs were top of Division One. Peter McWilliam, who masterminded their FA Cup win, went to the board to ask for money to shore up the side. The board refused. In December, the disillusioned McWilliam was offered £1,500 a year to manage Middlesbrough. He went back to the Spurs board and said he would stay if they raised his salary from £850 to £1,000. The board refused. One relegation and three failed managers later, the Spurs board asked McWilliam to come back.

10. Erik Thorstvedt v Nottingham Forest, 15 January 1989, Division One
Whether you see it as a Nigel Clough goal that snuck through Thorstvedt's hands or a ball he dropped into his own net, the debut clanger became part of the Erik the Viking legend.

11. Lee Dixon, Arsenal v Tottenham, 11 May 1991
Dixon had a habit of trying to lob Dave Seaman with his back passes – maybe he even gave Nayim the idea – so this 40-yard pearler of a lobbed own goal should come as no surprise really. Pity the Gooners won 6-1.

> "THAT'S THE FIRST TIME I'VE CHIPPED A BALL ALL SEASON."
> MABBSEY AFTER HIS CUP-FINAL CLANGER

PLAYERS WHO WERE FANS

From fan to first team

1. Arthur Rowe
2. Tony Marchi
3. Ron Henry
4. Jimmy Greaves
5. Terry Venables
6. Jimmy Pearce
7. Glenn Hoddle
8. Mark Falco
9. Teddy Sheringham
10. Sol Campbell
11. Luke Young

PLEATYISMS

"I was sitting just a few feet away from David Pleat at the World Cup. He's a nice fellow but the man is mad, certifiably, eye-spinningly mad." Danny Kelly

1. "I was inbred into the game by my father."

2. "Our central defenders Doherty and Anthony Gardner were fantastic and I told them that when they go to bed tonight they should think of each other."

3. "The man we want has to fit a certain profile. Is he a top coach? Would the players respect him? Is he a nutcase?" Pleaty wants to sign his antithesis as next manager.

4. "That is a real cat-and-carrot situation."

5. "Apart from John Terry, Chelsea are a team of immigrants. Where are the players like Veron now? Is he still alive? Where's Petit and where's that full-back from Holland. What's his name? Bogarde. Is he still making films? I feel sorry for [Ranieri] because he is something of a gypsy and Chelsea have kept him out of the picture." David Pleat on the Roman revolution.

6. "There's Thierry Henry, exploding like the French train that he is."

7. "If there are any managers out there with a bottomless pit, I'm sure that they would be interested in these two Russians."

8. "He hits it into the corner of the net as straight as a nut."

9. "Lizazaru…Lizeru… Lizazu…Lizru…Lirezu…."The 1998 World Cup was a nightmare for Pleaty

10. "For such a small man Maradona gets great elevation on his balls."

11. "When you finish playing football, young man – which is going to be very soon, I feel – you'll make a very good security guard." David Pleat to Neil Ruddock, then 17.

"FOR SUCH A SMALL MAN, MARADONA GETS GREAT ELEVATION ON HIS BALLS." PLEATY ON TOP FORM

QUICK OFF THE MARK

11 players who impressed from the first whistle

1. In 1898 Ken McKay scored on his debut in four different categories: a friendly (a hat-trick), the Thames and Medway League, the United League and the FA Cup.

2. James Hartley scored both Spurs' goals on his debut against Gravesend United in a 2-0 win on 9 October 1897.

3. Charlie Wilson scored all three goals of the game on his league debut away to South Shields in the Second Division on 20 September 1919.

4. Les Bennett scored a hat-trick on making his Spurs debut in a war-time league match. Spurs beat Watford 8-2.

5. Jimmy Greaves scored three on his Spurs debut in a 5-2 win against Blackpool.

6. Alfie Conn's hat-trick inspired Spurs to a 5-2 win at Newcastle on his full debut.

7. Glenn Hoddle made his debut at 17 and scored in Spurs' 2-1 win over Stoke City.

8. Within two days of joining Spurs, Colin Lee scored four of Spurs' goals without reply against Bristol Rovers in Division Two on 22 October 1977.

9. Garry Brooke got two from midfield as a 20-year-old debutant against Southampton on Boxing Day 1980. The game finished 4-4.

10. Mido scored twice and played a blinder in his 2005 debut against Portsmouth.

11. Dean Marney scored two spectacular goals against Everton on his full home debut, 1 January 2005.

RECORD ATTENDANCES: ALL GROUNDS

All-time highest attendances

1. 114,815 Spurs 3 Sheffield United 1, FA Cup final, 20 April 1901 (Crystal Palace)
2. 100,000 Spurs 2 Leicester City 1, FA Cup final, 6 May 1961 (Wembley)
3. 100,000 Spurs 1 Liverpool 3, League Cup final, 13 March 1982 (Wembley)
4. 100,000 Spurs 2 Chelsea 1, FA Cup final, 20 May 1967 (Wembley)
5. 100,000 Spurs 1 QPR 1, FA Cup final, 22 May 1982 (Wembley)
6. 100,000 Spurs 3 Burnley 1, FA Cup final, 5 May 1962 (Wembley)
7. 100,000 Spurs 1 Manchester City 1, FA Cup final, 9 May 1981 (Wembley)
8. 98,000 Spurs 2 Coventry City 3, FA Cup final, 16 May 1987 (Wembley)
9. 97,446 Spurs 1 Norwich City 0, League Cup final, 3 March 1973 (Wembley)
10. 97,024 Spurs 2 Aston Villa 0, League Cup final, 27 February 1971 (Wembley)
11. 95,000 Real Madrid 0 Spurs 0, UEFA Cup r4, 2nd leg 20 March 1985 (Bernabéu)

RECORD ATTENDANCES: HOME

11 highest at the Lane

1. 75,038 Spurs 0 Sunderland 1, FA Cup 6th round, 5 March 1938
2. 71,913 Spurs 1 Preston North End 3, FA Cup 5th round, 6 March 1937
3. 71,853 Spurs 3 West Bromwich Albion 1, FA Cup 4th round, 24 January 1948
4. 70,882 Spurs 2 Manchester United 0, Division 1, 22 September 1951
5. 70,347 Spurs 1 Bolton Wanderers 1, FA Cup 5th round, 16 February 1935
6. 70,302 Spurs 4 Southampton 0, Division 2, 25 February 1950
7. 70,026 Spurs 7 Newcastle United 0, Division 2, 18 November 1950
8. 69,821 Spurs 1 Arsenal 4, Division 1, 10 October 1953
9. 69,781 Spurs 1 QPR 0, Division 2, 16 October 1948
10. 69,265 Spurs 0 Southampton 1, Division 2, 2 April 1949
11. 69,247 Spurs 1 Arsenal 3, Division 2, 20 September 1952

RECORD TRANSFERS

A mixed money-bag

Record	Fee	Player	From	Date
Club record	£1,700	Fanny Walden	Northampton	Apr 1913
Record for a full-back	£21,000	Alf Ramsey	Southampton	May 1949
Record for a half-back	£30,000	Danny Blanchflower	Aston Villa	Dec 1954
Record for a winger	£35,000	Cliff Jones	Swansea	Feb 1958
National record	£99,999	Jimmy Greaves	Milan	Dec 1961
Record for a half-back	£72,500	Alan Mullery	Fulham	Mar 1964
Record for a defender	£95,000	Mike England	Blackburn	Aug 1966
National record	£125,000	Martin Chivers	Southampton	Jan 1968
National record	£200,000*	Martin Peters	West Ham	Mar 1970
Club record	£2.9m	Gheorge Popescu	PSV Eindhoven	Sep 1994
Club record	£4.5m	Chris Armstrong	Crystal Palace	1995

*Includes part exchange

RESURRECTIONS

11 classic comebacks

1. Dave Mackay

The crowd heard Mackay's leg crack when Noel Cantwell clattered into it. It had twisted 90 degrees. It could well have ended there. A year on, a reserve game against Shrewsbury Town was the first step back. Mackay was standing on his healed leg when a boot hammered into the back of it and broke it again. He weightlifted, he dieted, one more year passed and in a 4-2 win against Leicester in August 1965 he was back again. Inspirational as ever. But there was one more comeback in him yet. Three years on and feeling the pace, he told Bill Nick his time was up. Brian Clough was less sure and spirited him off to Derby to become Footballer of the Year.

2. Gornik Zabrze, European Cup 1st round, 1962

An hour into their all-new European adventure Spurs were 4-0 down. The Katowice ground was packed with 100,000 Poles, Gornik were packed with internationals and Spurs were at sea. Terry Dyson and Cliff Jones's goals clawed back a lifeline. Back at Spurs, the crowd never stopped roaring and Spurs never stopped scoring. Cliff Jones bagged the perfect hat-trick and Spurs rampaged to a magnificent 8-1 win.

3. Alan Mullery

Mullery's injury was labelled "a pelvic strain", but no one really knew. Indefinite rest was the only care. When he got finally through it he couldn't get back in the team. But then a good old-fashioned Spurs injury crisis struck. On the brink of the UEFA Cup semi-final against Milan, Bill Nick recalled Mullery and he clinched the tie with a 20-yard volley at the San Siro. In the return leg of the final at White Hart Lane he clinched the UEFA Cup, knocking himself out scoring the winning header.

4. 1919/20 season

What can you do when the Gooners gets you thrown out of the First Division? Win 32 matches, score 102 goals and get promoted right back up again. Then finish above the Gooners in your first season back. Classy.

5. Ossie Ardiles

It was only one more season of nigh-on vintage Ossie, but after his Falklands War exile, a cartilage operation and two broken legs, 1986/87 was some kind of miracle.

6. Everton 1937 FA Cup fifth round replay

Spurs were 3-1 down with six minutes to go and facing a penalty. But the linesman had spotted a foul throw: no penalty. Just time for Jimmy Morrison to score his second, Joe Meek to equalise and Jimmy Morrison to complete his hat-trick.

7. Keith Burkinshaw's Spurs

Two FA Cups, a UEFA Cup and two fourth-place finishes within six seasons of being promoted. That's bouncebackability.

8. David Copeland

After his injury against Newton Heath it all looked over for David Copeland. Walsall let him go and he signed for Bedminster. But he battled back. On joining Spurs he won the Southern League in 1899/90 and the FA Cup the season after.

9. 6-2 v Southampton

Two-nil down to the Saints on a weekday night in the fourth round of the Cup. These are the times you wonder why you bother. Two goals in two minutes, four in extra time and a stonking Rocket Rosenthal hat-trick provided a timely reminder.

10. Jürgen Klinsmann

Jürgen broke the never-go-back rule and for a time it seemed rash. Until those four goals in the 6-2 win over Wimbledon in April 1998 saved our Premiership bacon.

11. In reverse

Spurs have always had a talent for collapses. Witness: Burnley in 1960 (4-0 up, drew 4-4), Aston Villa in March1966 (5-1 up, drew 5-5), Manchester United in September 2001 (3-0 up, lost 5-3) and Manchester City in February 2004 (3-0 up, lost 4-3).

ROGUES AND SCOUNDRELS

The clown princes

1. Paul Gascoigne

Arch-rogue, joker, moron, alcoholic… Gascoigne hits every note between endearing and exasperating. When he treated the camera to a close-up of his tonsils after scoring the 1991 FA Cup semi-final free kick, it was all part of the moment. When he tricked a Spurs supporter into climbing onto the roof of a camper van, which he then drove up the A1, everyone apart from the supporter thought it was hilarious. When he fractured his knee in a nightclub after his desperately needed big-money transfer to Lazio had already been jeopardised by his cruciate injury, Spurs were less impressed. When he downed quadruple Drambuies at a team lunch in the run-up to the 1991 FA Cup final, it was the start of something altogether more desperate.

2. John White

White's humour veered towards the surreal: taking a chrysanthemum from a vase and casually snacking on it was a favourite trick. He and Jones were the clown duo of the Double team. After the European Cup game at Benfica, Bill Nick was hauled out of bed by the hotel manager who said the players had started a fight. He found Jones and White fencing with swords that had been hung on the hotel wall. With earnest enthusiasm, White explained that he was a huge Robin Hood enthusiast.

"Did you know that when Robin Hood lay on his deathbed he asked for his bow and arrow to be brought to him?" White asked the bemused Nick. "He told Little John and Maid Marion he wanted to fire his bow one last time and wherever the arrow landed, that was where they should bury him."

"Where did they bury him?" asked Bill, interested, despite the circumstances and the late hour.

"In the ceiling."

> HE FOUND JONES AND WHITE FENCING WITH SWORDS THAT HAD BEEN HUNG ON THE HOTEL WALLS

3. Cliff Jones

"I wouldn't do what those dogs do, for love nor money," said one of the Spurs players as the team stood watching a police dog team complete an assault course as part of the pre-match entertainment before a game at Nottingham Forest. "I would. I'll do it for a quid from each of you," replied Cliff Jones. Jonesy's £10 was well earned: not a tunnel nor plank was omitted as, still in his civvies, Jones nipped round the course with his typical tricky winger agility.

4. Dave Mackay, Terry Venables, Jimmy Greaves and Cliff Jones

As the Double team broke up, the jokers regrouped. Assistant boss Eddie Bailey was the comical quartet's favourite victim. They engaged the apprentices to rush over to Bailey with a phone message: "Your brother Bill called to say he won't be coming home." The more it wound Eddie up, the more they did it.

5. Cyril Knowles

If ever there was a sharp one-liner to be had, Knowles was on to it. New signings all suffered initiation at Knowles's hands. When he terrified the fans by dummying and swerving past opponents in the most dangerous situations, you sensed it was all just another Knowles practical joke.

6. Phil Beal

The pictures in the papers showed Phil Beal, together with Geoff Hurst, Rodney Marsh and Franny Lee accessorised with frilly shirts and cigars, trying for all they were worth to look like glam playboys. Not a tabloid sting, but a publicity gimmick. They called themselves The Clan and the plan was to sell their image. That was Phil Beal off the pitch. On it, he was cautious and dependable; in the dressing room he was the laugh-a-minute man perking up the team.

7. Roger Morgan

The 1970s winger was one of the team clowns and admitted to modelling himself on George Best. He had the Best hair and the Best rogue in him, but somewhat less of the skill and none of the drive. He hadn't come cheap at £110,000 from QPR and was described at one point as Bill Nick's most expensive mistake. "Every team needs a joker," said Eddie Bailey in *The Glory Game*. "Is that why you bought Roger?" replied a voice in the dressing room.

8. Joe Kinnear

As if Knowles, Morgan and Beal were not enough for one side, Kinnear was another with an over-developed sense of humour. "But I don't smoke. I've told you. I don't smoke," he said repeatedly to an unfortunate Romanian hotel official who was trying to convince Kinnear to fill in his passport number. This was the rigorous age of the Iron Curtain, but enough is enough and the official gave up and went away.

9. Alfie Conn

Conn was more moody rogue than loveable clown. The typical temperamental talent, Alfie turned it on when he felt like it and played where he wanted, not where the manager told him. Sitting on the ball (see Absolute Best Moments) was typical, if wonderful, Conn arrogance. Terry Neill recalls accompanying him before an FA disciplinary committee in the hope of getting a charge reduced or revoked. Tie-less and hippy-haired, Conn began to mutter and grumble during the hearing and was subsequently unsuccessful in his appeal.

10. Terry Naylor

When Naylor turned pro with Spurs in 1969 he turned up to his first training session with the words: "Anyone fancy dying today? Cos if they do, they should tackle me." His stint as a Smithfield Market porter cultivated his cheeky sense of humour.

11. Neil Ruddock

Ruddock once admitted to holding his wife's head under the covers when he farts.

SCANDALS

11 tales of bribery and corruption

1. Trial of the century

On 14 May 1993, Alan Sugar and his cronies sacked Terry Venables as Spurs' chief executive. Venables brought an injunction to reverse the board's decision pending a full hearing. The private rot might have set in long before, but that's when the public dirty-laundry exercise began. The allegations and counter-allegations of corruption were unending; militant fans in masks hung off lamp posts outside the Royal Courts of Justice to abuse Sugar; others turned up to picket his home. Few remember what it was all about; just that a promising spurt of football had been stunted once again.

2. Irving Scholar and the story of the dodgy loans

The FA called it a breach of the "regulations dealing with the avoidance and evasion of fees". Mitchell Thomas, Paul Allen, Chris Fairclough, Paul Gascoigne and Chris Waddle had been given loans on joining Spurs under the Irving Scholar regime. Loans are not liable for tax. Trouble was, they were never meant to be re-paid. Spurs were dealt a 12-point deduction, a ban from the FA Cup and a £600,000 fine. Swindon, who had been demoted after being found guilty of a similar offence, were unimpressed, even more so when Sugar's crack lawyers got all but the fine lifted.

3. Bunging

"What usually happened in these cases was people would meet Mr Clough in a motorway café and Mr Clough would be handed a bag full of money." Alan Sugar claimed that was what Terry Venables told him about how Cloughie did business. The alternative story runs thus: a company called First Wave undertook transfer negotiation and marketing work for Spurs over the course of a year or so. Frank McLintock of First Wave was Teddy Sheringham's agent. When McLintock met Venables on the day the Sheringham deal went through he was unhappy First Wave still had not been paid for previous work. He said if Spurs wanted the Sheringham deal completed they must pay First Wave that day. The money that changed hands was payment for services rendered by First Wave and not destined for the Cloughie wallet. On this, Brian Clough, Teddy Sheringham and Terry Venables are agreed.

4. Panorama Special

Normally, special editions of *Panorama* are about General Elections and wars. But in 1993 there was one on Terry Venables. The crux of its allegations was that Venables took a backhander from Gino Santin, the man who represented Spurs in the transfer of Gazza to Lazio. A fee was paid to Santin to negotiate Gazza's price up from the £4.825m Lazio wanted to pay to the £5.5m Spurs valued him at. The issue centred on a fax from Lazio that already offered £5.5m. If Venables had seen this fax, the implication was that Santin's involvement was unnecessary. It suggested that part of Santin's £200,000 fee might have gone into Venables's pocket. Venables is adamant the fax (addressed to Irving Scholar) was never shown to him.

5. Backwards crawl

In 1987, Spurs finished third in the league, reached the FA Cup final and the semi-finals of the League Cup. Naturally there was only one way forward: self-implosion. A national newspaper made allegations about David Pleat's private life. Pleat survived that but was sacked when the charges resurfaced.

6. Paynegate

Ernie Payne couldn't get a game for Fulham, so when Spurs asked him to come and play in their London Senior Cup tie against Old St Marks in October 1893 he was happy to accept. But Ernie contrived to mislay his kit on the way to Spurs' Northumberland Park ground. The club provided socks, shorts and a shirt, but had no boots to fit. Payne was given ten shillings to buy a pair that would belong to the club. Within ten days, Spurs were harshly punished by the Football Association for offering an "unfair inducement" – professionalism. The incident persuaded the board it might be an idea to actually go professional.

7. The case of Tommy Lunn
Poor Tommy Lunn was only doing what comes naturally to footballers. In 1913 he took out a publican's licence. The Spurs board were none too impressed and it was in breach of Lunn's contract, so they suspended him.

8. Durie's out
In 1992, Gordon Durie got into trouble for an even more common footballing predilection. Coventry's Andy Pearse had appeared to head butt Durie, who supposedly tried to use his persuasive skills to convince the referee contact had been made. Durie was charged by the FA and banned for three games for trying to get his fellow pro into trouble. The decision was later reversed on appeal.

9. Trouble at the YMCA
Kind local Bible reader John Ripsher secured the use of the local YMCA basement as Tottenham Hotpur's first permanent HQ. The rascally Spurs boys repaid him by getting themselves chucked out. The hullabaloo of a basement knockabout was disrupting a YMCA committee meeting above. When a venerable member chose to investigate, the light was turned out and he received a well-struck ball in the face.

10. Trouble at t' Church
When Spurs were chucked out of the YMCA, Ripsher found them a home at 1 Dorset Villa, Northumberland Park, a branch of the Young Men's Church of England Society. But the Rev Wilson would only let Spurs use the premises if the boys came to church every Wednesday. The arrangement worked swimmingly until Mr Wilson discovered them running a card school among the pews during service. The long-suffering Ripsher then found them rooms in the Red House on Tottenham High Road. They contrived to behave themselves for the next 120 years: the Red House now houses the press office.

11. Push off and run
Imagine if David Dein began lambasting Arsenal's style of play in the matchday programme and advocating a return to offside traps and long-ball tactics. Imagine it, not just because it would be highly amusing, but because a similar thing

happened at Tottenham at the start of the 1950s. Manager Arthur Rowe's new, passing, push-and-run game had taken Spurs to the Second and First Division titles in successive seasons. But directors Eddie Dewhirst Hornsby and Bill Herryet were nostalgic for the good old kick-and-rush days. They did everything they could to undermine push-and-run, talking up the old-style game in their programme notes. The pressure of their niggling combined with the stress of deteriorating results finally drove Rowe to resign due to a nervous breakdown.

SCAREDOS

Dodgy highlights and perms

1. Ralph Coates Like one of those dolls you buy at airports with glued-on hair that comes unstuck. Hinged at the left, it came on and off like a lid.

2. Chris Waddle There are mullets and there's what Chris Waddle had. Short and upright on top with a flap at the back. Like one of those Foreign Legion hats.

3. Alfie Conn Huge 'tache, long voluminous barnet, sideboards that needed feeding.

4. Phil Holder Such a shame his haircut never got more games for Spurs. It came in three bits: a shoulder-length curtain either side, and a left-to-right sweep-over.

5. Tim Sherwood Had several different styles, every one a girl's haircut.

6. Maurice Norman Big Mo was taller in his hair. Hair was always sensible in the 1960s but Norman looked like the kid at school whose mother cut it once a year.

7. Gazza The one that was skinhead until an inch above his ears and skullcap on top.

8. Alan Brazil Bald and bubbly.

9. Micky Hazard Just bubbly.

10. Gerry Francis Darts-player chic.

11. Paolo Tramezzani Shoulder-length curtains.

> TIM SHERWOOD HAD SEVERAL DIFFERENT STYLES – EVERY ONE A GIRL'S HAIRCUT

SEASONS TO FORGET

11 reasons to be tearful

1. 1914/15 Bottom of Division One with just eight wins from 38 games and 90 goals shipped. Relegation (when World War 1 was over) would have been avoided if it weren't for Arsenal's skulduggery.

2. 1927/28 Spurs finish 21st in Division One, leaking 86 goals, and are relegated.

3. 1929/30 Spurs' achieve their lowest-ever finish in the Football League – 12th in Division Two – and exit the FA Cup in the third round.

4. 1930/31 Third in Division Two: Spurs miss out on promotion by one place and three points and have to endure two more seasons in Division Two.

5. 1934/35 Bottom of Division One: Spurs go back down after only two seasons.

6. 1955/56 18th in Division One; Spurs concede ten more goals than they score.

7. 1958/59 Spurs finished third in 1957/58 but in Bill Nick's first season they drop to 18th and go out of the FA Cup in round six to Third Division Norwich City.

8. 1974/75 19th in the league and out of the FA and League Cups in the third and second rounds respectively.

9. 1976/77 Bottom and relegated. Out of the FA and League cups in the third round.

10. 1991/92 Good runs in the League and Cup Winners' Cups, but still struggling to get out of Scholar's financial black hole. Dropped down the league, finishing 15th. Peter Shreeve resorted to direct football and Lineker's goals propped the team up.

11. 2003/04 Hoddle is sacked after a six-game stay of execution and the rest of the season is spent playing mediocre football under a caretaker manager.

SEASONS TO REMEMBER

Make it a Double

1. 1960/61 Honours: League title, FA Cup

The season began with an 11-game winning run. Spurs played such glorious attacking football they were dubbed the Team of the Century. League form dipped as their FA Cup run progressed but soon revived when they beat Burnley in the semi-final. The title was clinched with a 2-1 win against nearest challengers Sheffield Wednesday on 17 April. Spurs lost two of their last three league games, but still finished eight points clear. "We all believed strongly that if people spent their hard-earned money coming to watch a football match, they deserved to be entertained," says Dave Mackay. The FA Cup final didn't quite live up to the ideal as Leicester were beaten 2-0 but Spurs were the first side to win the Double in the 20th century. When Bill Nicholson took over just 30 months earlier they had been fighting relegation.

2. 1962/63 Honours: Cup Winners' Cup

Spurs' 1962 FA Cup win qualified them for the Cup Winners' Cup and they were drawn to face Rangers in the first round. Spurs went into the first leg as championship leaders, with 19 more goals to their name than any other club. Rangers were beaten 5-2 at White Hart Lane and 2-0 in the return, despite a lot of Scottish bravado. When the competition resumed in March, Spurs made light of Slovan Bratislava and the dirty tactics of OFK Belgrade, winning the ties 6-2 and 5-2 on aggregate. Their league form suffered between the European games, but they still finished second, six points behind Everton. They went out of the FA Cup in the third round, losing 3-0 to Burnley, but the Cup Winners' Cup final was rich consolation: a 5-1 win in one of the greatest games Spurs have ever played.

3. 1961/62 Honours: FA Cup

This season was all about the glory glory nights: the floodlit European Cup games and their incredible atmosphere as 60,000 voices joined in singing *Glory Glory Hallelujah*. Playing in their all-white strip, Spurs dispatched Gornik Zabrze, Feyenoord and Dukla Prague before going out to Benfica in an incredible semi-final. The only addition to the Double side was Jimmy Greaves, who arrived in December and scored 30 goals in the remainder of the season. But the European Cup had its effect on Spurs' league form and, despite a strong run-in, they finished third, four points behind champions Ipswich Town. In the days before the UEFA Cup, an FA Cup win was the only way to get another bite at Europe. After Birmingham took them to a replay in the third round, Spurs found the rest of their Cup run easy, including the final, when Burnley were dispatched 3-1.

4. 1950/51 Honours: League title

Spurs lost their first game 4-1 to Blackpool, who seemed to have discovered a way to foil their push-and-run tactics. Results continued to be mixed until the end of September. Was the revolutionary style that saw Spurs storm Division Two ineffective at the top level? An eight-game winning run that began with a 3-2 victory over Aston Villa and ended with a 7-0 trouncing of Jackie Milburn's Newcastle suggested not. Manchester United emerged as Spurs' only threat, but with a game to go, a 1-0 win over struggling Sheffield Wednesday sealed the title.

5. 1981/82 Honours: FA Cup

In March, Spurs were on for the Quadruple. They played 65 competitive games over the season and at one stage, Spurs fans had a cup tie to go to every week. It was quite some centenary season. The fixture backlog made league success virtually impossible but fourth place was still Spurs' best finish in ten years and good enough to qualify for the UEFA Cup. Spurs lost a major final for the first time to Liverpool in the Milk Cup and went out of the Cup Winners' Cup to Barcelona in the semi-final. Only the FA Cup remained. After war broke out in the Falklands neither Ardiles nor Villa played. The final and replay (won with a Hoddle penalty) against QPR were dire games, but at least there was some silverware to show for an epic season.

6. 1971/72 Honours: UEFA Cup

Bill Nick's side had come again. There weren't quite the goals, glory and the romance of the 1960s – as Bill Nick never tired of reminding Mullery, Chivers, et al – but, in the season after Arsenal had bored their way to the Double, Spurs put together a majestic UEFA Cup campaign. They put 15 past the Icelanders from Keflavik, squeezed past Nantes, outclassed Rapid Bucharest 5-0 on aggregate and snuck past Romanian side Unizale Textile Arad. Then came Milan. At White Hart Lane, Milan snatched a goal on the counter and sat back. Long-range goals were the only answer and Steve Perryman produced two beauties. A magnificent draw in Milan took Spurs through to an anti-climatic final and Wolves were dispatched 3-2. Runs to the sixth round of the FA Cup, the semi-finals of the League Cup and sixth place in the league completed the campaign.

7. 1986/87

Out went Peter Shreeve, along with Mark Falco, Paul Miller and Graham Roberts. In came David Pleat, bringing Richard Gough, Mitchell Thomas, Steve Hodge and Nico Claesen. Clive Allen scored 49 goals as the lone striker in front of a fluid five-man midfield. It was Glenn Hoddle's last season at Spurs and by March the Treble was still on. After two legs and a replay, David Rocastle won the Littlewoods Cup semi-final for Arsenal in the last minute. The push for the title was choked with cup ties – Spurs finishing third. The FA Cup looked set to provide consolation. It was a fantastic final, but Mabbutt's extra-time own goal won it for Coventry.

8. 1949/50 Honours: Division 2 champions
Arthur Rowe's push-and-run football was simply unstoppable. Spurs opened the season with three 4-1 victories, then, after losing 3-2 to Blackburn, embarked on a seven-game unbeaten run. They played 22 games between the end of August and the end of December and dropped just four points, all of them in draws. They led Division Two from start to finish. With the title won, they eased up and lost four of their last five games, yet still finished nine points clear of Sheffield Wednesday.

9. 1980/81 Honours: FA Cup
This was where it all began to turn. After just three seasons back in Division One, Keith Burkinshaw had fashioned another great side for Spurs. This was the one season where Garth Crooks and Steve Archibald truly clicked, scoring 47 goals between them, with Glenn Hoddle adding 15 from midfield. Spurs finished tenth in the league, but only three of the sides above them scored more goals (though of course none let as many in). It was all about the FA Cup, though. QPR, Hull, Coventry and Exeter were beaten in the early rounds. Spurs looked set for a comfortable 2-1 win over Wolves in the semi-final before referee Clive Thomas awarded Wolves a penalty after a well-timed Hoddle tackle outside the area. The injustice motivated Spurs to take Wolves apart 3-0 in the replay. The 100th FA Cup final was billed as a beauty and the beast encounter, with Spurs pitched against a hardworking Manchester City side, but in the end it was all beast – a dull 1-1 draw. The replay was worth the wait though, Spurs winning a thrilling game 3-2, with Ricky Villa scoring one of Wembley's greatest ever goals.

> **CLIVE ALLEN SCORED 49 GOALS AS THE LONE STRIKER IN FRONT OF A FLUID FIVE-MAN MIDFIELD**

10. 1889/90
On 28 April 1890, a huge crowd was milling outside Bruce Grove station, waiting for Spurs to return from New Brompton where they had clinched the Southern League title on the last day of the season. The Tottenham Town Band led a procession back to the clubhouse. Nothing like it had been seen in Tottenham before. It was the club's first season at White Hart Lane. With their entertaining style, they were christened the Flower of the South.

11. 1994/95
There were no trophies, no European games, but 1994/95 was pure Tottenham:

glory, drama and despair in equal measure. It began with Spurs having been deducted 12 points, banned from the FA Cup and fined £600,000. On the bright side, there were three World Cup stars and a five-man forward line. Goals were scored and goals were shipped and Ossie Ardiles had to go. Gerry Francis arrived and Spurs rose to an unlikely seventh-place finish. Alan Sugar's lawyers got Spurs' points back and restored them to the Cup and fate and the form of Jürgen Klinsmann said it had to be Tottenham's year. There was Ronnie Rosenthal's hat-trick against Southampton and the amazing quarter-final win at Anfield. But injuries hit and Spurs crumpled 4-1 against Everton in the semi-final. The World Cup stars all left and the following season banality returned.

SUGAR WAS NEVER SWEET

11 tasty quotes from Alan

1. "I know more about schmaltz herring than I do about football."

2. "Double? What Double? Is that something from the 1950s?"

3. "Bugger off. If you think I'm in it for anything other than money, you can ask my family."

4. Sugar: "Who's that geezer over there?"
[Terry Venables explains it's Nick Barmby, one of Spurs' most promising youngsters]
Sugar: "Well, flog him. That'll pay for the South Stand."

5. "Venables ain't put in as much money as me. Why are they chanting his name instead of mine?"

6. "I'll just get another geezer in." Alan Sugar to Terry Venables on being asked who he'll get to replace El Tel as manager.

7. "I feel like the man who shot Bambi. I don't know what all the fuss is about. Managers come and go." To the press after sacking Venables.

8. "I wouldn't wash my car with that shirt." Sugar on Klinsmann.

9. "You've got to be f**king joking if you think you're going to spunk my money all over the wall." At a board meeting to discuss signing new players.

Other Sugar gems included:

10. Getting the club fined 100,000 Swiss francs for knowingly allowing Spurs' friendly against Lazio to be televised, thus promoting the interests of Sky, whose dishes were manufactured by Amstrad.

11. Generally running a football club like, well, an apprentice.

TALES OF THE TRADE

11 jobs outside football

1. Mining

Cyril Knowles worked down a Yorkshire mine for three years. He'd virtually given up on football when Middlesbrough came in for him. A season later Bill Nick picked him up for £45,000. Willie Evans, who was a star outside-left for Spurs in the 1930s, was working down the pits in Wales when Spurs snapped him up at 16.

2. Manufacture

Pat Jennings worked as a factory hand on leaving school at 15, while Ron Henry worked for the Empire Rubber Company at the same age. Joe Kinnear worked as a machine-minder for 18 months before turning professional. Before Hearts, Dave Mackay was an apprentice joiner.

3. Electrical

Danny Blanchflower and Bill Brown were both apprentice electricians while Chris Hughton signed for Spurs after completing his training as a lift engineer.

4. Other sports

Clive Allen tried his hand as a kicker for the London Monarchs after giving up football. 1921 FA Cup-winning centre-forward Jimmy Cantrell became a professional golfer. Fanny Walden became a test-match umpire. Cliff Jones turned to teaching PE. Alan Gilzean spent three years as a bookie before turning to football.

5. Press
Push-and-run centre-forward Len Duquemin ran a newsagents on Northumberland Park, while Double-winning keeper Bill Brown worked for a letter press and lithograph printers, later owning his own business. Producing the copy were football journalists John Cameron, an early playing and managerial great, 1940s manager Joe Hulme, who quit Spurs to work for the *People*, and the endlessly eloquent Danny Blanchflower.

6. Fashion
Goalkeeping great Ted Ditchburn ran a successful men's outfitters in Romford after a brief bash at management. Maurice Norman owned a wool shop and winger Jimmy Pearce owned a ladieswear business.

7. Transport
Martin Peters ran a car insurance firm with Bobby Moore. Jimmy Dimmock, scorer of the winning goal in the 1921 cup final, worked in road haulage in later life. While playing for Spurs Martin Chivers was a 'sales rep' for Leford Motors in Epping. Peter Shreeves qualified as a London cabbie before joining Spurs' coaching staff. John Cameron quit Everton for Spurs because his team-mates were averse to him working in the Liverpool offices of the Cunard shipping line.

8. Builders/property/home and garden
1950s and 60s wing-half Toni Marchi went into wallpapering after a spell in management, later working in the building trade. Jimmy Pearce owned a builders' merchants, Joe Kinnear owned a property company and was director of a furniture shop while at Spurs. Bill Brown moved to Canada and worked in real estate, and later for the land development section of the Ontario government. His team-mate Ron Henry owned a plant nursery until 2003.

9. Sports shops
Both Alan Mullery and Steve Perryman owned sports shops.

10. Timber
Pat Jennings was a labourer in a timber gang until he was 17. He was soon playing for Spurs, alongside Mike England, who owned a timber firm.

11. Catering
Cyril Knowles owned a fish and chip shop during his Spurs days, while Cliff Jones opened a family butchers on White Hart Lane.

TEAMS WE HATE

They're just a bunch of whingers and bad sports

1. Arsenal See Teams We Really Hate: Arsenal.

2. Chelsea Because they're a small team in Fulham. And they stole our billionaire.

3. West Ham For being near our patch. Though it's more condescension really: they take our cast-offs, we take their best players.

4. Leeds They were hard when they didn't need to be; they had great players but were still dirty. Also, Gooner David O'Leary was their ever-whingeing manager.

5. Southampton It's mostly them doing the hating after we poached their manager and centre-back. Hoddle was returning to a situation of mutual worship and in relieving them of Dean Richards for £8.1m we were more than generous.

6. Fulham They went crawling to the FA in 1893 just because one of their reserves turned out for us and we bought some boots for him to play in (see Scandals). The Cottagers' actions got Spurs banned from playing for two weeks and saw them thrown out of the Amateur Cup.

7. Feyenoord Old European foes. Spurs have met them four times in the UEFA Cup and the Cup Winners' Cup. Wins and losses stand at two each, but Feyenoord triumphed in the 1974 UEFA Cup final, when Spurs fans rioted after having a goal disallowed. Feyenoord are traditionally anti-Semitic (to this day some fans persist in making hissing noises in imitation of the gas chambers) and hate Ajax, a club, like Spurs, with strong Jewish support.

8. Rapid Bucharest December 1971, UEFA Cup third round: "It was the dirtiest team I've seen in 30 years. If this is European football, I'd rather have a Football Combination match. Diabolical." Such were Bill Nick's words after the game in Bucharest. Rapid needed to score four goals to win, and had decided not to bother trying, concentrating instead on damage-maximisation. Alan Gilzean was punched in the kidneys and subjected to a Cantona-kick; Steve Perryman's shoulder was dislocated in a bad tackle, and Gilzean and Peter Collins needed their ribs strapped. All this by half-time. And in the second-half, it got worse.

9. Pre-World War 1 German teams By 1913, Britain was not Germany's favourite country, which became clear on the German leg of a European tour. The football was

TERRY VENABLES 1991 FA CUP WINNERS

Erik Thorstvedt

Gary Mabbutt   Steve Sedgley
Pat van den Hauwe   Justin Edinburgh

David Howells

Vinny Samways   Nayim
Paul Stewart

Paul Allen   Gary Lineker

They could be heroes – just for one day... This is the side after Gazza went off, a side which Venables said had a better balance than the one that started the final

brutal and the fans savage. In one match a fan split goalie Tiny Joyce's head open with an umbrella to the unbridled glee of the crowd. Chairman Roberts vowed never to visit Germany again, a promise the club kept until years after his death.

10. Barcelona April 1982 European Cup Winners' Cup semi-final. It's the same as Leeds, only worse: if you're Barcelona why would you want to play dirty football and grind out a result? A lily-livered referee stood by as the Spaniards kicked Spurs around in their own backyard. Things scarcely improved at Camp Nou, as Barça clung grimly to the 1-0 lead they had fluked at White Hart Lane.

11. Lyon November 1967, European Cup-Winners' Cup second round, first leg. Lyon decided they would bully their way through and the Czech referee couldn't be bothered to disagree. Finally, Alan Mullery retaliated after being kicked in the face. An eight-minute brawl ensued before Mullery and his aggressor were sent off. Spurs escaped with a 1-0 deficit, but handed the tie to Lyon at White Hart Lane after scorning numerous chances to finish them off.

TEAMS WE REALLY HATE: ARSENAL

11 for now but there are hundreds more

1. They invaded our patch. Spurs shelled out £50,000 on the West Stand in 1909. As the only club of any stature in North London, this was a sound investment. Until Arsenal chairman Henry Norris decided to move his Woolwich club in next door.

2. They got us chucked out of Division One. Spurs had finished bottom in 1914/15, but Division One was due to be expanded by two clubs. The last time this happened, no teams were relegated. But it seems that Henry Norris leaned on various people and when a ballot was held at a league meeting in 1919, Arsenal, who had finished sixth in Division Two, were voted into Division One at Spurs' expense.

3. ...thus killing our parrot. On the ship back from the 1909 South American tour two players dressed up as Robinson Crusoe and Man Friday, complete with parrot. It became a Spurs pet until it died of grief shortly after that fateful meeting in 1919.

4. They allegedly threw games in an effort to get Spurs relegated in 1927/28.

5. Boring football. Herbert Chapman's WM formation turned the course of English football to defence. In 1970/71 the Gooners won the Double, proving that anything you can do playing fabulous football you can do boring the pants off people too.

6. Dubious moral character. Need we say more.

7. Their shameless luck. The 1987 League Cup semi-final: two legs and a replay. Arsenal won it, having led the tie for just one minute out of the whole five hours.

8. Pat Rice's arse. So they won 5-0 at our place in 1978. An eloquent form of 'up yours' you might think, but Rice still felt the need to display his bare behind to all.

9. Thuggery. Paul Davis broke Glenn Cockerill's jaw during a league game in 1988.

10. More thuggery. Ian Wright was banned for three games after aiming a punch at David Howells during the game at the Lane in August 1993.

11. Cheating. In a 1999 FA Cup fifth round tie the Sheffield United keeper kicks the ball into touch so his injured team-mate can receive attention. Ray Parlour neglects to return the ball to a startled United side and Overmars scores. Okay, they did replay the tie but their base instincts were obvious.

THANKS A MILLION

The first 11 Spurs to leave for a million big ones or more

1. **Glenn Hoddle**   £1m   Monaco
2. **Steve Archibald** £1.5m   Barcelona
3. **Clive Allen**   £1m   Bordeaux
4. **Chris Waddle**   £4.25m   Marseille
5. **Richard Gough** £1.5m   Rangers
6. **Vinny Samways** £2.2m   Everton
7. **Paul Stewart**   £2.3m   Liverpool
8. **Paul Gascoigne** £5.5m   Lazio
9. **Steve Sedgely** £1m   Ipswich
10. **Gordon Durie** £1.2m   Rangers
11. **Nick Barmby**   £5.25m   Middlesbrough

THEY PLAYED THE GAME OF THEIR LIFE!

He played a blinder

1. **Charlie Walters** 1921 FA Cup final
2. **Ron Henry** 1961 FA Cup final
3. **Bill Brown** 1963 Cup Winners' Cup quarter-final first leg v Slovan Bratislava
4. **Terry Dyson** 1963 European Cup Winners' Cup final
5. **Neil Johnson** v Manchester United (h) October 1965 (Spurs won 5-1)
6. **Joe Kinnear** 1967 FA Cup final
7. **Martin Peters** 1973 UEFA Cup semi-final second leg v Liverpool
8. **Tony Parkes** 1984 UEFA Cup final
9. **Paul Stewart** 1991 FA Cup final
10. **David Ginola** FA Cup fifth round replay v Leeds
11. **Allan Nielsen** 1999 Worthington Cup final

TOP APPEARANCES

11 greatest servants of the club

		League	FA Cup	League Cup	Europe*	Total
Steve Perryman	1969-86	653 (2)**	69	66	63 (1)	851 (3)
Pat Jennings	1964-77	472	43	39	36	590
Gary Mabbutt	1982-98	458 (19)	45 (2)	60 (2)	22 (3)	585 (26)
Cyril Knowles	1964-75	400 (1)	42	32 (1)	30	504 (2)
Glenn Hoddle	1975-87	370 (7)	47 (1)	44	17 (4)	478 (12)
Ted Ditchburn	1946-58	418	34			452
Jimmy Dimmock	1919-31	400	38			438
Alan Gilzean	1964-74	335 (8)	40	27 (1)	27 (1)	429 (10)
Phil Beal	1963-75	330 (3)	30	27	30	417 (3)
Maurice Norman	1955-65	357	37		17	411
Mike England	1966-75	300	32	30	35	397

*Does not include Anglo-Italian Cup Winners' Cup
**Substitute appearances in brackets

TOP LEAGUE GOALSCORERS IN A SEASON

11 best in their year

Goals	Scorer	Season	Club total	League position
37	**Jimmy Greaves**	1962/63	111	2nd
36	**Bobby Smith**	1957/58	93	3rd
36	**Ted Harper**	1930/31	88	3rd, Division 2
33	**Clive Allen**	1986/87	68	3rd
33	**George Hunt**	1932/33	96	2nd, Division 2
32	**George Hunt**	1933/34	79	3rd
32	**Bobby Smith**	1958/59	85	18th
31	**Bert Bliss**	1919/20	102	1st, Division 2
29	**Jimmy Greaves**	1964/65	87	6th
28	**Bobby Smith**	1960/61	115	Champions
28	**Gary Lineker**	1991/92	58	15th

TOP SCORERS

11 best in their time

		League	FA Cup	League Cup	*Europe	Total
1. Jimmy Greaves	1961-70	220	32	5	9	266
2. Bobby Smith	1955-64	176	22		10	208
3. Martin Chivers	1968-76	118	11	23	22	174
4. Cliff Jones	1958-68	135	16	1	7	159
5. George Hunt	1930-37	124	13			137
6. Len Duquemin	1947-57	114	20			134
7. Alan Gilzean	1964-74	93	21	6	13	133
8. Teddy Sheringham	1992-97/ 2001-03	97	14	13		124
9. Les Bennett	1946-54	104	14			118
10. Jimmy Dimmock	1919-31	100	12			112
11. Glenn Hoddle	1975-87	88	11	10	1	110

*Not including Anglo-Italian Cup

TOP WEBSITES

Spurs in cyberspace

1. Jim Duggan's Top Spur Site (www.topspurs.com). Often slow to load, but has sound editorial comment, previews, match reports, trivia, history, Arsenal-bashing.

2. My Eyes Have Seen The Glory (www.mehstg.com). Comprehensive, not sexy.

3. Spurs Odyssey (www.spursodyssey.com). Match reports are the Odyssey forte: first-team, reserves, youth – all sizes and descriptions.

4. News Now (www.newsnow.co.uk and choose Spurs from the dropdown football menu). Collates news stories, rumours and gossip from all over the internet.

5. The Evening Standard (www.thisislondon.co.uk and go to Sport, Football and choose Spurs). Good quality stories.

6. Sky Sports Spurs Home Page (http://skysports.planetfootball.com). Good news stories (but some may remind you of what you read on the official site).

7. THFC 1882 (www.thfc1882.com) Slick, and a good all-rounder.

8. The Spur (www.thequake.com/thespur.html). Good for stories and reaction.

9. Team Talk (www.teamtalk.com and select Spurs from the dropdown menu). Okay for catching up after you've been on holiday.

10. Glory Glory (www.glory-glory.net). Good considered opinion and stats.

11. The Bill Nicholson Way (www.billnicholson.co.uk). Cyber shrine to Sir Bill.

WEST HAM: THE SECOND SPURS REJECT BIN

If we don't hand them straight over, they eventually wash up there anyway

1. Jimmy Greaves	Spurs: 1961-70	West Ham: 1970/71
2. Clive Allen	Spurs: 1984-88	West Ham: 1992-94
3. Chris Hughton	Spurs: 1979-90	West Ham: 1990-91
4. Mitchell Thomas	Spurs: 1986-1991	West Ham: 1991-94
5. Neil Ruddock	Spurs: 1986-88	West Ham: 1998-00
	Spurs: 1992-93	
6. Ilie Dumitrescu	Spurs: 1994-96	West Ham: 1996-97
7. Teddy Sheringham	Spurs:1992-1997	West Ham: 2004-present
	Spurs: 2001-03	
8. Sergei Rebrov	Spurs: 2000-04	West Ham: 2004-present
9. Matthew Etherington	Spurs: 1999-2003	West Ham: 2003-present
10. Bobby Zamora	Spurs: 2003-04	West Ham: 2004-present
11. Maurizio Taricco	Spurs: 1999-2004	West Ham: 2004-present

WHAT'S IN A NAME?

Spurs players with odd, intriguing or silly monikers

1. Baden Herod (or Edwin Redvers Baden Herod to give him his full name)
A record £4,000 buy from Brentford in 1929, the full-back played only 59 games.

2. Bert Badger
The centre-half/centre-forward guested in nine games for Spurs in 1904/05.

3. Bert Bliss
Inside- or centre-forward, 1921 FA Cup final winner scored 168 goals in 315 games.

4. Albert Hall
Welsh utility player who scored 21 goals in 81 games for Spurs, 1935-47.

5. Willie Newbigging
The centre-forward was a regular in 1896/97, Spurs' first Southern League season.

6. Lycurgus Burrows
Also mercifully known as Ly, Burrows signed from Woolwich Arsenal in 1894. The tough-tackling full-back played 119 games before moving to Sheffield United.

7. Pat Gilhooley
The Lanarkshire-born inside-forward scored seven goals in 50 games for Spurs after arriving from Sheffield United in 1901. He moved on to Brighton in 1904.

8. Walter Bugg
The Arsenal reject centre-half joined in 1902, playing just one game.

9. Cuthbert Monk
Monk couldn't decide whether he was a half-back, full-back or a goalkeeper, but seemed to do best between the sticks, playing there in Spurs' first FA Cup tie in 1894.

10. Harry Crump
Began at Smethwick Centaur and several Midlands clubs before coming to Spurs for a season in 1896. He went to Luton but was back in 1899 for 105 more appearances.

11. George Foreman
A centre-forward/inside-forward with a powerful shot, Foreman scored 39 goals in 56 appearances between 1946 and 1949 when he was ousted by Len Duquemin.

WONDER GOALS

11 glorious strikes

1. Ricky Villa: Spurs 3 Manchester City 2, 1981 FA Cup final replay Wembley
Back in Spurs' half, not far from the area. Tony Galvin pushed the ball to him. The crowd
waited for extra time. But Villa waited for no man, least of all City defenders. He
swerved inside, outside, drew goalkeeper Joe Corrigan and dummied to shoot before
slotting home. Three-two. It was the 100th FA Cup final and Wembley's finest goal.

2. Paul Gascoigne: Spurs 3 Arsenal 1, FA Cup semi-final 14 April 1991
They had to give Gazza an injection to knock him out the night before the game.
When he woke the next day he was still too hyper to put his mind to anything for
even a nanosecond. But when Spurs won a free kick 35 yards out, his concentration
was complete. If he simply bent the ball it would be saved. It would need to have
pace. Swerve and true pace are hard to combine. But before Seaman had time to
time to say "venomously struck curler" the ball was in the net behind him.

3. Jimmy Greaves: Spurs 5 Man United 1, Division One 16 October 1965
Between the centre-circle, where Greaves received the ball from Alan Mullery, and
the goal were five United players. Greavsie danced past every one and walked the
ball in. He did almost exactly the same against Leicester twice, once in 1962, when
Gordon Banks was in goal, and again in 1968, when Peter Shilton was the victim.

4. Glenn Hoddle: Spurs 3 Oxford 1, Division One 25 April 1987
Hoddle began in his own half. The Oxford defence tried to play offside, a ruse Hod
rumbled by passing to himself, chipping the defence and picking the ball up on the
other side. He dummied, leaving the keeper on his backside, and slotted home.

5. Martin Chivers: Spurs 2 Wolves 1, UEFA Cup final, first leg 3 May 1972
This game needed glamour badly. It was the first leg of a European final, but it was at
Molineux. The football was turgid. With the game at 1-1, Chivers produced the spark.
Knowles overlapped and passed to Mullery, who passed to Chivers. He would surely
hold the ball up. Or else turn, accelerate, beat two men, and thunder the ball into the
far corner from at least 30 yards out. Which is what he decided to do.

6. David Ginola: Barnsley 0 Spurs 1, FA Cup quarter-final 16 March 1999
It was cold, it was a Tuesday night, it was Barnsley in front of 19,000 people. But
David Ginola scored a goal for a Cup final. He made light of a four-man Barnsley
slalom course to calmly slot home and take Spurs into the FA Cup semi-final.

7. Jürgen Klinsmann: Spurs 1 Southampton 1, Premiership 10 May 1998
An otherwise meaningless fixture against Southampton. But this was Mabbutt's last day and Klinsmann's second and final farewell. The crowd roared its gratitude and Klinsmann returned the compliment: a stunning goodbye volley.

8. Les Allen: Spurs 2 Sheffield Wednesday 1, Division One 17 April 1971
An unsung Double-winner. His spectacular waist-high volley sealed the win over Sheffield Wednesday. The title was clinched. All eyes turned to the FA Cup final.

9. Cyril Knowles: Spurs 2 Man United 1, Division One 10 November 1973
Cyril Knowles picked this goal as his finest moment in football. It was a sweet, curling free kick that swung around United's goal and into the top corner.

10. Stephen Carr: Spurs 3 Manchester United 1, Premiership 23 October 1999
Two-one up against Man U, 20 minutes to go. The crowd craved the scalp of the Treble-winners. Steve Carr found the ball in his own half, carried it upfield and hammered past Mark Bosnich from 30 yards. His strike was voted goal of the season.

11. Pat Jennings: Spurs 3 Manchester United 3, Charity Shield 12 August 1967
Dave Mackay had been about to take a free kick, when Jennings called to knock it back. Jennings drop-kicked it, aiming for Alan Gilzean. Alex Stepney came out to claim but the ball missed Gilly, missed the stranded Stepney and bounced in. The game was a thriller, but as Stepney laments, it's only ever remembered for one thing.

WORST DEFEATS (BY MARGIN OF DEFEAT)

11 days to have left before the final whistle

1. 0-7 v Liverpool (a)	2 Sept 1978	League
2. 2-8 v Derby (a)	16 Oct 1976	League
3. 1-7 v Newcastle (a)	28 Oct 1996	League
4. 6-0 v Sunderland (a)	21 Feb 1934	League
5. 6-0 v Arsenal (h)	6 Mar 1935	League
6. 6-0 v Leicester City (a)	28 Mar 1935	League
7. 6-0 v Sheffield United (a)	2 Mar 1993	League
8. 2-7 v Liverpool (a)	31 Oct 1914	League
9. 2-7 v Newcastle (a)	1 Sept 1951	League
10. 2-7 v Blackburn (a)	7 Sept 1963	League
11. 2-7 v Burnley (a)	21 Apr 1964	League

X-FILES

Totally random trivia – from baseball to Zamalek

1. For a while, in the 1960s, for reasons that are still mysterious, three fans dressed up as angels would appear at home games at White Hart Lane.

2. In 1906 and 1908 Spurs won the British Baseball Cup.

3. Real Madrid toured Britain in 1924/25 and were beaten 4-2 by Spurs Reserves.

4. Olympic hurdler Donald Finlay played three games for Spurs on the right wing.

5. Terry Venables was named after Terry's chocolates.

6. Dave Mackay could toss a coin, catch it with his foot, flick it up and catch it on the back of his neck, catch it on his foot again, flick it up and catch it in his breast pocket.

7. On 8 December 1973, a mere 14,034 fans turned out to watch Spurs beat Stoke City 2-1, the club's lowest league attendance in the last 50 years.

8. Terry Neill used model cowboys and Indians to illustrate his team talks.

9. When Spurs beat Southampton 4-2, all four Spurs goals were scored within four minutes and 44 seconds.

10. Mido's signing has merely boosted Spurs' popularity in Egypt. In 1962 Spurs beat Zamalek 7-3 in a friendly. The Egyptians regard this as Zamalek's finest hour.

11. The name Hotspur originates from Shakespeare's character Harry Hotspur. He was based on a member of the aristocratic Northumberland family who owned lots of land in Tottenham, and the club's first ground was located just behind the Northumberland Arms pub.

THE YEAR ENDED WITH A ONE: WHERE IT ALL STARTED

It was Spurs' inter-passing game against Sheffield United's kick-and-rush, and 115,000 people wedged into the Crystal Palace ground to watch. The Cutlers had nine internationals but Spurs' passing game prevailed, after a replay.

1. George Clawley, goalkeeper
Within a month of arriving in May 1899, George Clawley broke his leg. Good in the air and comfy with long-range shots, he'd helped Southampton to two Southern League titles. But he dropped two clangers in Spurs' FA Cup run. At Reading in the fourth round, Sandy Tait punched off the line after Clawley had fumbled. The ref's view was blocked and Spurs walked the replay. In the final Clawley dropped it again. This time the ball trickled wide, the linesman pointed for a corner, but the referee was pointing to the centre-spot. Sheffield United had scored a phantom equaliser.

2. Harry Erentz, full-back
Signed from Newton Heath in 1898, the Scot known as Tiger tackled fiercely and gave nothing away. When Spurs went a goal down to Sheffield United in the replay, he and Sandy Tait held them together. Spurs released Erentz in 1904, and he was out of the game altogether after breaking his leg playing for Swindon.

3. Sandy Tait, full-back
Terrible Tait's speciality was a mean-but-fair sliding tackle. If his legs were a little slow, his brain was one of the quickest. Football was his passport out of the Ayrshire pits, and the Scot became a renowned full-back in six years at Preston before joining Spurs. He made a formidable captain near the end of his nine years at the club.

4. Ted Hughes, centre-half (midfield)
The 1901 FA Cup run made Hughes's career. Two years after his move from Everton, he was still a reserve. But when captain James McNaught was injured, Hughes took his place for the third-round replay at Preston and made himself indispensable. Small, but good in the air, he had energy to burn and liked to support his forwards.

5. **Tom Morris**, right-half

Tom Morris anchored his half-back line when others strayed forward and was ever-present in the 1901 Cup campaign. When Spurs entered the Football League in 1908/09 he was the only FA Cup winner still at the club.

6. **John L. Jones**, left-half

It wasn't Ardiles or Klinsmann, but Jack Jones's transfer from Sheffield United in 1897 was a coup. He was a Welsh international; Spurs were just a Southern League team. He brought intelligence and skilful passing, and his half-back line began to boss the play against his old club as the 1901 replay drew on. He was the first Spur to represent his country and the first Spurs captain to lift the FA Cup.

7. **Tom Smith**, right-winger

High, dipping crosses for centre-forwards' heads, pull-backs for inside-forwards and searing pace made up the Smith armoury. In the 1901 final replay he set up the first goal and scored the second. In 1902 he bizarrely retired at the age of 25.

8. **John Kirwan**, left-winger

When the whistle blew in Bolton, Kirwan seized the ball and kept it until he died in 1959. Spurs' first Irish international had all the tricks. A fast-paced flyweight winger given to embarrassing the lumbering defenders of the day, he passed and crossed with aplomb and developed a lethal telepathy with inside-left David Copeland.

9. **Sandy Brown**, centre-forward

Brown was an identikit centre-forward, a penalty-box poacher. He wasn't tall but often scored with his head (as he did from a corner in the replay). He is still the record FA Cup top-scorer in a season with 15 goals – including a hat-trick against Preston, all four against West Brom in the semi-final and a brace in the final.

10. **John Cameron**, inside-right

Player-manager John Cameron was a playmaker, talented dribbler and pass master. Once a centre-forward, his scoring knack didn't leave him at inside-right. After Spurs began to flounder in the final replay he had wingers Kirwan and Smith cut inside to exploit the space behind Sheffield United's full-backs. Cameron scored the equaliser.

11. **David Copeland**, inside-left

With a cannonball right-foot shot and an aggressive edge, Ayrshire-born David Copeland scored a goal every three games for Spurs in 302 appearances. At just 5ft 7in and weighing less than 12 stone, he had surprisingly been a centre-forward. At Spurs he switched to inside-left from where he set up many a Sandy Brown goal.

YOU CANNOT BE SERIOUS

Disallowed (or not allowed) goals

1. Jimmy Greaves v Benfica 1962 European Cup semi-final first leg. Referee Poulson disallowed Greavsies' perfectly good-looking goal which would have allowed Spurs to equalise within a minute of Benfica's opener.

2. Bobby Smith v Benfica 1962 European Cup semi-final, first leg. The ball actually passed two Benfica players on the way to the net, but the linesman flagged offside – after the referee had blown his whistle for the goal.

3. Jimmy Greaves v Benfica 1962 European Cup semi-final, second leg. Greaves appeared to pull back a first goal for Spurs. Again referee Poulson blew his whistle for the goal. Again the linesman flagged.

4. Cliff Jones v Manchester City April 1960. Spurs came third this season, three points behind Burnley, but who knows what might have been if they'd got a result here. Spurs were awarded a penalty and Cliff Jones took it. Bert Trautmann saved brilliantly but Jones slammed the ball home. The referee didn't give it because some time between the ball rebounding and Jones striking, he'd blown for half-time.

5. Chris McGrath 1974 UEFA Cup final, second leg. It had finished 2-2 at the Lane and after 20 minutes in Rotterdam Chris McGrath had a goal disallowed for offside. Shameful rioting from the Spurs following ensued. It's hard to escape the conclusion this contributed to Bill Nick's feeling of disillusionment. He resigned later that year.

6. Pedro Mendes v Manchester United January 2005. The famous goal that was a yard and a half behind the goal line not given. As Fergie might say, sinister!

7. Gary Lineker v Nottingham Forest 1991 FA Cup final. Lineker timed his run perfectly to meet Paul Allen's cross. The linesman's judgement was less perfect.

8. Cliff Jones v Leicester 1961 FA Cup final. Spurs won the Double despite having a legitimate Cliff Jones goal called offside five minutes before half time at 0-0.

9. Jimmy Banks v Preston 1921 FA Cup semi-final. Banks goal for Spurs was disallowed because of an earlier foul – on Spurs player Jimmy Seed.

10. Goalmouth scramble v Preston 1921 FA Cup semi-final. The ball ended up in Preston's net but the referee disallowed it and gave a free kick.

11. Bert Bliss v Preston 1922 FA Cup semi-final. Bliss smashed his shot through the net but the referee disallowed it, thinking there was a Preston player injured.

YOU CAN'T HAVE ONE WITHOUT THE OTHER

Great Spurs partnerships

1. Dave Mackay and Danny Blanchflower

Mackay and Blanchflower liked to attack, but knew instinctively when to cover each other. They spent hours mulling over tactics and moves. For the 1962 Cup final, Danny proposed that if Spurs won a penalty, he'd roll the ball forwards a couple of feet. When the goalkeeper dived, Mackay would put it the other side. With Spurs 2-1 up, a Burnley player handled in the box. Blanchflower looked at Mackay who lost his bottle, charging back into his own half leaving Danny to shimmy and score.

2. Glenn Hoddle and Ossie Ardiles

"They were the odd couple who talked the same language," says team-mate Paul Miller. Hoddle's long game and Ossie's short passes; Hoddle's grace and Ossie's nippiness; Hoddle's string-pulling and Ossie's reading of the game.

3. The G Men: Jimmy Greaves and Alan Gilzean

In their first game together Gilzean set up two goals for Greaves. With his positional awareness, selfless game and perfectly directed knockdowns, Gilzean was perfect for Greaves who said: "I don't think I was ever happier than when playing with Gilly."

4. Martin Chivers and Alan Gilzean

Martin Chivers could throw a football pretty much as far as he wanted, and Alan Gilzean could head one in any direction or place or at the speed he chose. Lethal.

5. Jürgen Klinsmann and Teddy Sheringham

Klinsmann said Sheringham was the best strike partner he ever had. Sheringham said: "If I never play with a better footballer than Jürgen Klinsmann I will have been a lucky man," which probably means the same thing. They scored 52 goals between them in 1994/95. In the FA Cup quarter-final win over Liverpool, Klinsmann set up Sheringham for the first, Sheringham flicked to Klinsmann for the second. Poetic.

6. C&A: Garth Crooks and Steve Archibald

"That first season there was something magical about them," says Keith Burkinshaw. But after 1980/81 the magic began to evaporate. Then there was the team divide.

You were either with Archibald or against him. Crooks was with him, Hoddle was against. "[Crooks and Archibald] protected each other," says Steve Perryman. "They convinced each other they were both right and in truth they were both wrong."

7. Alf Ramsey and Ted Ditchburn
In the 1940s and 50s goalkeepers weren't supposed to be thoughtful distributors of the ball. This made little sense to push-and-run Spurs boss Arthur Rowe. Ditchburn became the first line of attack, pioneering the short throw with right-back Ramsey.

8. Richard Gough and Gary Mabbutt
It was a meeting of defensive minds, but a maddeningly short-lived one. Both had the skill and vision to leave the backline and go play, but their intuitive relationship meant the team was rarely left exposed.

9. David Copeland and John Kirwan
Copeland formed an irresistible partnership with Irish international winger Kirwan on Spurs' left flank, inspiring them to a Southern League championship in 1900 and the FA Cup in 1901. They moved together to Chelsea in 1905.

10. Tony Galvin and Chris Hughton
Tony Galvin and Chrissie Hughton had a pretty good thing going on Tottenham's left wing during the 1980s. Hughton was a skilful full-back who liked to get forward and Galvin a solid winger who was good at tracking back. Perfect.

11. Alan Sugar and Terry Venables
It was the "dream ticket", remember? The business supremo allied to the football man. And it staved off the threat of Robert Maxwell. Despite everything that happened afterwards, that may even have made it all worthwhile.